The Semi-Official Dallas Cowboys Haters' Handbook

Mark Nelson
and
Miller Bonner

The Semi-Official Dallas Cowboys Haters' Handbook

Collier Books
Macmillan Publishing Company
New York

Collier Macmillan Publishers
London

MACMILLAN PUBLISHING COMPANY
866 Third Avenue, New York, N.Y. 10022
Collier Macmillan Canada, Inc.

Library of Congress Cataloging in Publication Data

Nelson, Mark, 1949–
The semi-official Dallas Cowboys haters' handbook.

1. Dallas Cowboys—Anecdotes, facetiae, satire, etc.
I. Bonner, Miller, 1950– . II. Title.
GV956.D3N44   1984   796.332′64′0976422812   84-10072
ISBN 0-02-029440-9

Macmillan books are available at special discounts
for bulk purchases for sales promotions, premiums,
fund-raising, or educational use. Special editions
or book excerpts can also be created to specifica-
tion. For details, contact:

Special Sales Director
Macmillan Publishing Company
866 Third Avenue
New York, New York 10022

10 9 8 7 6 5 4 3 2 1

Printed in the United States of America

"Try to tell the truth in Dallas and you'll find some frozen hemlock in your nachos."
—*CBS announcer Tom Brookshier*

Contents

Acknowledgments

The idea for this book came to us one spring day in 1983 as we sat in Timberlake's Restaurant savoring the best onion rings on Capitol Hill.

We had seen a similarly titled book about a baseball team in a nearby bookstore window, but agreed the author had the wrong team.

As Texas reporters, we never adopted the Cowboys as our favorite football team. It seemed only natural that we launch this crusade.

Most of the people we talked to liked the idea, but warned we were treading on dangerous turf. "The Cowboys—and most of their fans—don't have a very good sense of humor," one friend warned.

But the more we talked about it, the more we decided it was the right thing to do.

We owe stadium-sized thank-yous to a number of people who helped us. First among them are Brooke Ramey Nelson and Karen Bonner, who put up with late-night phone calls and endless requests for copyediting, at which they did an excellent job.

We were extremely fortunate that the proposal fell into the hands of Jeff Neuman, whose enthusiastic support was of immeasurable help to two novices. He also suggested the book would read better if we used verbs.

Ron Goldfarb, an ardent Redskins fan, guided us skillfully through the legal maze of publishing.

Others who were very helpful include Mark Siegel, Jeanie Cavett and Barnee Breeskin.

Pete Gent gave the world *North Dallas Forty* and *The Franchise*, and he gave us candid assessments of the Cowboys and Tom Landry.

We had fun researching anecdotes about the Cowboys that we found in a variety of places including: Bob St. John's *Landry*; Bob Lilly's *Bob Lilly: Reflections* (with Sam Blair); Richard Whittington's *The Dallas Cow-*

boys; Carlton Stower's *Journey To Triumph*; Sam Blair's *The Dallas Cowboys—Pro or Con?*; Steve Perkins' *Next Year's Champions*; Lou Sahadi's *Super Sundays* and *The Washington Redskins*; Jerry Kramer's *Instant Replay*; George Allen's *Football's 50 Greatest Games* (with Ben Olan); Tim Panaccio's *Cowboys an' Indians*; Roger Staubach's *Time Enough to Win* (with Frank Luksa); John Thorn's *The Armchair Quarterback*; Frank Deford's *Lite Reading*; Bert Randolph Sugar's *The Book of Sports Quotes*; and *The Official NFL Encyclopedia of Pro Football*, compiled by the NFL.

In addition, we thank the sportswriters and broadcasters who chronicled the Dallas Cowboys on and off the field for such publications as *Sports Illustrated, Inside Sports, D Magazine, Texas Monthly, Pro, Esquire, Hustler, Playboy, The New York Times, The Washington Post, The Dallas Morning News, The Dallas Times-Herald, The St. Petersburg Times,* and *USA Today*.

We owe a debt of gratitude to many others, but they agreed to cooperate with us only if we allowed them to remain anonymous.

—*Mark Nelson & Miller Bonner*

Introduction

If you get nothing else from the pages of this book, at least remember this: the Dallas Cowboys are not "America's Team." The Cowboys, if the truth be known, are about as popular with real Americans as Exxon and AIDS. Hating "America's Team" has become a national pastime. Come to think of it, what could be more American than hating the Dallas Cowboys?

Nothing.

Yet the Cowboys have managed to hoodwink an unsuspecting public. They have created and perpetuated the Big Lie that the Dallas County Corporates are the most awesome, wholesome, powerful, prayerful, popular football team ever to strap on helmets.

That myth is fed weekly by the television networks, chiefly CBS (the Cowboys Broadcasting System), which beams those dreadful silver-and-blue uniforms into our living rooms every Sunday. Sometimes the networks give us a break on Sunday only to wreck our Monday night, and they even have the audacity to spoil Thanksgiving by force-feeding us those Lone Star turkeys.

The media saturation has taken its toll. Misguided children in Boise, Battle Creek and Birmingham unwittingly force their parents to buy Cowboys pennants, posters, pencils, playing cards, helmets and mugs.

Oh, if those poor parents—and football fans everywhere—knew the TRUTH about those devils from Dallas, they would save themselves a lifetime of worshipping the team every true American loves to hate.

Think fast—how many Super Bowls have the Cowboys won? Six? Eight? Ten? Would you believe *two*? Well, what can you expect when the Greatest Living Cowboy, Roger Staubach, can't even spell r-e-l-i-e-f.

That's why we've set the record straight. To know the Cowboys is to hate them. And we know them only too well.

Forget the hype you've heard over and over again from Howard Cosell, Frank Gifford, Pat Summerall, John Madden, and Don Meredith (he was one of *them*, by the way, before he escaped).

Forget about "legendary" Landry, Bob Hayes, Tony Dorsett, and the Rolaids salesman.

Instead, remember the Madison Avenue propaganda that created a Cowboys myth as large as Texas— or Tex Schramm's ego.

Think of the obnoxious Dallas fans. The ones who arrive at Texas Stadium in their limousines. The big-mouth braggarts in boots and ten-gallon hats who think the world revolves around their crude oil and Cadillacs, their cattle ranches and Cowboys.

Why, those fraidycat footballers of the frontier aren't even from Dallas. They play in Irving. The Irving Cowboys. Ha! Try selling luxury boxes to see a team with a name like that!

Sure, their uniforms look like they were lifted from a jewelry store window. But if the Cowboys are so successful, so rich, so powerful, why can't they fix the hole in the roof of their stadium?

Real fans around Big D remember when Dallas might have had "America's Team." As in the American Football League. As in the Dallas Texans. As in Abner Haynes. Len Dawson. E. J. Holub. Now there was a football team.

Remember when the Cowboys told their field goal kicker *after* the season that the "pulled groin" injury he played with all season was really a hernia and he needed an operation?

That's Compassion.

That's Caring.

That's the Cowboys.

We've stripped away the sugar coating and revealed the naked truth (no offense, Mr. Rentzel) about the Cowboys. And we've recalled some classic Cowboys hate stories. And some classic Cowboys Haters.

Like the 1972 NFC Championship game in Washington when George Allen's Redskins slaughtered the Cowboys 26-3.

Or the Pittsburgh Steelers' memorable 35-31 victory over You-Know-Who in Super Bowl XIII.

And doesn't it send a chill of joy down your spine just thinking of the block Green Bay Packer guard Jerry Kramer threw on Cowboy tackle Jethro Pugh in the famous 1967 Ice Bowl?

Well, it's all here. Every crucial loss. Every unsightly blemish. Every embarrassment. From the All-Time Cowboy Killers to the Ring of Dishonor.

Enjoy the failures and the phonyism, the mistakes and the flops, the fumbles and the foibles of "America's Team."

Once you know the truth about the Cowboys and their boring, hypocritical organization, you'll feel cleansed. You'll be able to cite chapter and verse as to why America *really* hates the Chumps from Irving.

Arise America! Cowboys haters unite! We shall not walk alone.

The Semi-Official Dallas Cowboys Haters' Handbook

BUT FIRST, OUR NATIONAL ANTHEM

"Mammas Don't Let Your Babies Grow Up to Be Cowboys"
(with apologies to Willie, Waylon, and Ed and Patty Bruce)

Mammas don't let your babies grow up to be
Cowboys.
Don't let 'em sign contracts and play for those
dolts.
Make 'em be Redskins or Packers or Colts.
Mammas don't let your babies grow up to be
Cowboys.
They'll never have fun and they'll always be
shunned.
Even by people they love.

Cowboys are easy to hate, they're a lot worse
than sin.
They'd rather choke in the big games than try
hard to win.
Silver-blue helmets with great big ol' stars
Make you throw up wherever you are.
And if you really hate Dallas, you are not alone.
America walks by your side.

Mammas don't let your babies grow up to be
Cowboys.
Don't let 'em play football where nobody cares.
Make 'em be Falcons or Eagles or Bears.
Mammas don't let your babies grow up to be
Cowboys.
They'll never have fun and they'll always be
shunned.
Even by people they love.

Cowboys like computers and have robotlike
minds.
They think playin' like clones for plastic coaches
is fine.
Them that know 'em, won't like 'em a bit.
Them that do, won't ever admit it.
The Cowboys aren't winners, they're sorry old
chokes
And America knows it's the truth.

Mammas don't let your babies grow up to be Cowboys.
Don't let 'em play for Tom Landry and Texas E. Schramm.
Make 'em be Oilers or Steelers or Rams.
Mammas don't let your babies grow up to be Cowboys.
They'll never have fun and they'll always be shunned.
Even by people they love.

A History of Cowboy-Hating

Who were the first Dallas Cowboys haters?

Why, they were the good citizens of Big D who rooted for the best professional football team in town from 1960 to 1962—the Dallas Texans of the old American Football League.

Lamar Hunt, a maverick millionaire oilman from Dallas, was unsuccessful in his bid to get an NFL franchise for his hometown, so he found a novel way to bring professional football to Texas: he started his own league.

Once the NFL realized that Hunt had completed an end run around their opposition, they hurriedly voted to give a franchise to another Dallas oilman, millionaire Clint Murchison Jr., his brother, John, and Bedford Wynne. But it was too late: the AFL Texans were born. They would prove to be a burr under the Cowboys' saddle for years to come.

Both fledgling teams played their games at the Cotton Bowl, both teams had trouble drawing fans, both teams had trouble making money, but only one team had trouble winning.

The Cowboys began their life with a pitiful collection of castoffs, leftovers and retreads taken from the rosters of existing NFL teams, and they played like the charity cases they were. The Cowboys were so desperate to give their sparse crowds something to cheer that they invited Roy Rogers and Trigger to attend their first home game. The Cotton Bowl crowd not only booed the Cowboys, but a bunch of kids in the end zone seats threw ice at ol' Roy and his golden palomino.

This photo appeared in the first game program put out by the Cowboys. We're fairly sure that Roy, not Trigger, penned the inscription. ▲

Ah, but the Texans were different. Now there was a team you could cheer for: coach Hank Stram, Len Dawson, E. J. Holub, Abner Haynes, and Fred Arbanas. A team with character. A team with guts. A team that won.

While the Cowboys (who had initially been called the Rangers) were losing eleven games and tying one in their twelve-game maiden season, the Texans were winning eight, losing six.

In fact, the Cowboys' failures reminded a lot of fans of an earlier professional football team that played in Dallas, back in 1952. That team was also named the Texans. But these Texans may have been one of the worst teams to ever fumble a football. The 1952 Dallas Texans were, in fact, the old New York Yanks of the All-America Football Conference. When the AAFC folded, the NFL put the franchise in Dallas and renamed the team the Texans. From Yankees to Texans. You can imagine the joy in Big D.

The 1952 Texans, not the Cowboys, were the first football team in Dallas to wear silver, blue and white uniforms. In fact, the old Dallas Texans stationery looks remarkably similar to that of the Cowboys.

As you might imagine, Dallas never took to the Texans. Local high school and college football teams were more popular (and played better) and the Dallas Bible Belters thought allowing football on Sunday was as sinful as getting drunk, chasing women or playing the ponies.

The Texans lost their first game to the New York Giants 24–6 and went on to finish the season with a record of 1–11. They were pitiful, but they did win one more game than the 1960 Cowboys.

The original Dallas Cowboys Cheerleaders were the Cow Belles, who, unlike their modern-day counterparts, wore smiles and most of their clothes. ▲

By the end of that sorry 1952 season, it was evident that pro football didn't have much of a future in Dallas. Clint Murchison made noises about saving the franchise, but he was in South America when it came time to make a decision about the team.

So the Texans left Dallas for Baltimore where they were renamed the Colts and, fittingly, whipped the Cowboys in Dallas' first Super Bowl appearance.

But the AFL Texans of Lamar Hunt were a different breed. Their domination of NFL Cowboys was complete.

The Texans kept winning, the Cowboys kept losing. Off the field and on.

The lowly Cowboys even lost a milking contest to two AFL Texans in downtown Dallas during National Dairy Week.

IN THE BEGINNING WAS THE WORD, AND THE WORD WAS: DOORMAT

Here is the starting lineup for the Dallas Cowboys in their first regular-season NFL game against the Pittsburgh Steelers. The game was played in the Cotton Bowl on September 24, 1960.

Offense		*Defense*	
QB	Eddie LeBaron	DE	Nate Borden
HB	Don McIlhenny	DE	John Gonzaga
FB	Gene Babb	DT	Bill Herchman
WB	Frank Clarke	DT	Ed Husmann
E	Fred Dugan	LB	Wayne Hansen
E	Jim Doran	LB	Jack Patera
T	Dick Klein	LB	Tom Braatz
T	Bob Fry	CB	Tom Franckhauser
G	Duane Putnam	CB	Don Bishop
G	Buzz Guy	S	Billy Butler
C	John Houser	S	Fred Doelling

Here's the game-by-glorious-game account of that first season in which the Cowboys were outscored 369–186:

Pittsburgh 35	Dallas 28
Philadelphia 27	Dallas 25
Washington 26	Dallas 14
Cleveland 48	Dallas 16
St. Louis 12	Dallas 10
Baltimore 45	Dallas 7
Los Angeles 38	Dallas 13
Green Bay 41	Dallas 7
San Francisco 26	Dallas 14
Chicago 17	Dallas 7
New York 31	Dallas 31
Detroit 23	Dallas 14

The only Dallas running back to lead the league in rushing: Abner Haynes of the Dallas Texans led the AFL in 1960 with 875 yards. ▶

In 1961, the Cowboys won four games. The Texans won six. The following year, the Cowboys improved by one game and notched five victories.

The Texans, meanwhile, dominated the AFL, winning eleven games and the league championship in sudden-death overtime against the Houston Oilers.

In three years after professional football came to Dallas, the Texans' record was 25–17, including a league title. The Cowboys were 9–28–3.

But a funny thing happened.

Hunt looked at the bottom line of his football business and decided that Dallas had two chances of supporting two professional football teams: slim and none. (Of course, some folks thought the Texans *were* the only pro team in town.) He looked for greener pastures and found them in Kansas City. He moved his team and, perhaps with memories of the Cowboys, changed the name to the Chiefs. The Kansas City Chiefs would play in two Super Bowls, winning one, before the Cowboys could earn an invite.

The Cowboys continued to treat the people of Dallas in the fashion to which they were accustomed: they gave them still another losing season. It took the Cowboys until 1966 before they finally won more games than they lost.

BLACKMAIL TO THE REDSKINS

George Allen is usually credited with fanning the flames of the Cowboys-Redskins rivalry, but the real roots of the feud go back to the days when the Dallas Cowboys were a mere glint in the eyes of Clint Murchison.

George Preston Marshall, the legendary owner of the Redskins, opposed creating an NFL franchise in Dallas. He made no secret of his contempt for Murchison. But you don't make millions in the Texas oil business by backing away from a fight. The strong-willed Murchison, in a maneuver that would make J. R. Ewing look like a piker, found a way to offset Marshall's opposition. And he did it with Marshall's beloved fight song, "Hail to the Redskins."

Although several versions of the story exist, most everyone agrees that it all started with longtime Washington bandleader Barnee Breeskin, who composed the music to the song in 1938. Marshall's wife wrote the lyrics.

The plot thickened when Breeskin went through a divorce and retained the rights to "Hail to the Redskins." The bandleader wanted to turn his talents into some ready cash, but he didn't want to approach George Preston Marshall directly with such a request.

Instead, Breeskin contacted a Washington powerbroker named Tom Webb. One of Webb's clients was Clint Murchison. The story goes that a deal was arranged whereby Murchison bought the rights to "Hail to the Redskins."

In 1960 at the NFL meeting in Miami Beach, Murchison called Marshall and asked the Washington owner if he was planning to play "Hail to the Redskins" during the upcoming season.

Marshall said he would indeed play the song.

"Nobody," Murchison reportedly told him, "plays *my* fight song without *my* permission."

Marshall was understandably upset. But he was even more infuriated when Murchison told him the price for the return of his fight song: A "yes" vote at the league meeting for Murchison's Dallas franchise.

The deal was cut. Following two days of debate, Dallas was awarded an NFL franchise. The Cowboys were born.

Breeskin got $5,000 from Murchison. Marshall got his song back. And the NFL got its first glimpse of how the Cowboys do business.

★ GREAT PLAYS, MEMORABLE MOMENTS ★

In 1961, Cowboys owner Clint Murchison predicted the Cowboys would win eight to ten games and that 55,000 fans would watch Dallas play Cleveland for the conference championship. Clint's Cowboys finished the season 4–9–1.

As Dallas fans slowly warmed to the Cowboys, fans around the rest of the NFL began to despise them. Nowhere was such hatred more evident than in Green Bay territory. In the mid-1960s, hating the Cowboys was a more popular sport than skiing and deer hunting combined.

Vince Lombardi's Packers dominated the NFL during those years, but the sweetest victories were over the chicken-fried Cowboys in two straight NFL title games. Green Bay stomped Dallas six straight times before they let them win a game.

And if it wasn't the Packers, it was the Browns.

Cleveland got into the anti-Dallas spirit by waxing the Cowboys 11 out of 13 times between 1960 and 1966. Then the Browns intensified that hatred with two straight Eastern Conference championships over the Cowboys.

The word about the Cowboys was spreading around the country. Fans despised the Cowboys and everything they stood for because when Dallas won, it was never by enough points. And when the Cryboys lost, it was always the fault of the officials.

Cowboys Hate spread and made its way to our nation's capital. In 1971, hating the Cowboys was more important in Washington than hating Communists. Most Washingtonians felt the Cowboys posed the more serious threat to the nation's well-being.

And a Redskin coach named George Allen made sure no one ever forgot just how much Washington despised Dallas.

Allen's "Over-The-Hill Gang" beat Dallas 20–16 the first time they met and the fun began.

Allen knew how to play mind games with the Cowboys. He knew how to rile them up and he knew how to instill intense hatred of the Cowboys in his Redskins.

John Wilbur, a Cowboy offensive lineman from 1966 to 1969 who played for the Redskins from 1971 to 1973, told *Sports Illustrated* what effect Allen's hatred of Dallas had on the team.

"He cultivated it," Wilbur said. "It got to you. I mean he never referred to the Dallas Cowboys without calling them the goddamn Dallas Cowboys. I can't think of them as anything else now. My nine-year-old son, Nathan, even calls them that."

How does Wilbur feel about the Cowboys today?

"Well, just the sight of that silver-and-blue uniform inspires rage," he said.

The Dallas-Washington rivalry spawned a number of unforgettable moments: Lance Alworth throwing a crackback block on Jack Pardee; Harvey Martin throwing a black funeral wreath into the Redskins locker room; Diron Talbert making Roger Staubach cuss; Dexter Manley knocking Danny White unconscious in the 1983 NFC title game.

But it isn't just the fans in Green Bay, Cleveland and Washington who hate Dallas. Talk to someone in Pittsburgh or Denver or St. Louis or Philadelphia. They hate the Cowboys with a passion.

Dallas haters long for the day when Landry's cute little hat will blow off in a strong wind—and take his head with it. They dream about their favorite team's bludgeoning the beejeezus out of a team that has about as much soul as a fire hydrant.

Dallas haters go through life hoping, no, praying, that officials will have the guts to make the right calls against Dallas for a change, and know that if they do, the Cowboys will cry all the way back to Texas.

Dallas haters live for the day when the Cowboys will have the guts to admit to a big mistake and fix the hole in the roof of Texas Stadium.

Dallas haters don't care if Tom Landry leaves home without his American Express card just as long as he leaves; they're waiting for verification that the capital "C" on some of the Cowboys' uniforms stands for "candyass" or "crybaby."

As much as red-blooded Dallas haters universally admire beautiful women and as much as they love to ogle the Dallas Cowboys Cheerleaders, they can't help but wonder who pumps the air into their heads before each game.

Dallas haters despise the designer uniforms the

Cowboys wear. They love the legend of the unlucky blue jerseys and detest the little numbers the Cowboys have on their pants legs. (The pants legs shouldn't have numbers, they should have "left" and "right" on them.)

Happiness for a Cowboys hater would be putting Tex Schramm, Gil Brandt and Tom Landry on a raft and sending it out with the Japanese current.

Happiness for Dallas haters is learning that fans at Texas Stadium—the ones who "braved" the 27-degree temperatures (that's a heat wave in Green Bay)—booed Danny White and Landry and the rest of the overhyped Wowboys as they took the gas against the Rams in last year's playoffs.

What a fitting end to a Dallas season. Three straight losses. That's not history. That's heaven.

So let's toast the Dallas Cowboys:

> Here's to Dallas,
> Raise your glass.
> Here's to Dallas,
> Let's kick their ass!

Deflating the Myths

MYTH: *The Dallas franchise is one big, happy family.*
FACT: Even though Gil Brandt's ex-wife is married to former owner Clint Murchison, Jr., the Dallas Cowboys are as much one big happy family as the *Dallas* Ewings. Sure, we see Danny White and his family singing Christmas carols and the players plugging the United Way on television. Big deal. Let's get Thomas "Hollywood" Henderson, John Niland, Pete Gent and a few others together for a little Cowboys testimonial. Those players who question the motives of the Corporates get erased from the fans' memories pretty quickly in Dallas. Gent, author of *North Dallas Forty*, stopped getting invitations to the Cowboys alumni reunions. Now is that any way to treat a family member?

If anyone still thinks the Cowboys are a loving, caring, compassionate organization, consider what they did to one of their better players, Rayfield Wright. The big offensive tackle was one of the Cowboys' brightest stars for thirteen years. He had been voted All-Pro four times, played in six Pro Bowls, and all he wanted to do was finish his career with his beloved Cowboys.

But after Wright had a serious knee injury in 1979, the Cowboys decided his playing days were over. But did the Corporates give him an opportunity to retire gracefully? Are you kidding? Landry refused even to invite Rayfield to training camp in 1980 and put him on waivers. Then Rayfield retired. A number of Cowboys thought management had treated one of their all-time greats very shabbily.

MYTH: *The Cowboys are the best-paid team in the NFL.*

FACT: Given all the national television time and all the trinkets that are sold to their fans around the country and around the world, you would think the Cowboys

would share the wealth with the players. Dream on, Virginia. The "C" in Cowboys also stands for cheap. The Dallas brain trust isn't about to let dollars flow to the hired hands. *The Dallas Morning News* reported in 1982 that the Cowboys paid 31 of their 53 players less than the NFL average salary.

MYTH: *Tom Landry is a coaching genius.*

FACT: Okay, give the devil his due. Landry invented the 4–3 defense, the NFL standard for many years. But only a handful of teams still use it today. And, in case you haven't noticed, it hasn't worked for Dallas very well lately. In 1983, Dallas ranked 10th in the NFC in total defense, 13th against the pass, and 3rd against the rush. Dallas fans might blame Danny White for the team's failure to win the big games over the past four seasons, but remember who calls the plays: Tom Landry, the coaching genius.

★ GREAT PLAYS, MEMORABLE MOMENTS ★

Penalty-free football is a byproduct of superior coaching. The Cowboys hold Super Bowl records for most penalties in a game (twelve versus Denver in 1978); and most yards penalized (131 against Baltimore in 1971).

MYTH: *Dallas invented the scouting and free-agent formula that helped make the Cowboys so successful.*

FACT: Cowboys president Tex Schramm "borrowed"

1983 base salaries by position, including the league average, the highest salary in the league, plus the high and low salaries of the Cowboys. Being *America's Team* doesn't necessarily mean being America's best-paid team, does it?

POSITION	NFL AVERAGE	NFL HIGH	DALLAS HIGH	DALLAS LOW
Quarterback	$198,393	$600,000 Archie Manning, Minnesota & John Elway, Denver	$550,000 Danny White	$165,000 Glenn Carano
Running Back	$118,958	$890,000 John Riggins, Washington	$400,000 Tony Dorsett	$55,000 Gary Allen
Receivers (includes Tight Ends)	$104,699	$330,000 Harold Carmichael, Philadelphia	$225,000 Drew Pearson	$50,000 Cleo Simmons
Defensive Line	$111,302	$400,000 Lee Roy Selmon, Tampa Bay	$300,000 Randy White	$75,000 Bryan Caldwell
Offensive Line	$114,527	$432,000 Dave Rimington, Cincinnati	$235,000 Herb Scott	$50,000 Brian Bladinger
Linebackers	$104,238	$500,000 Tom Cousineau, Cleveland	$260,000 Bob Bruenig	$60,000 Angelo King
Defensive Backs	$97,153	$350,000 Louis Wright, Denver	$175,000 Everson Walls	$50,000 Bill Bates

the idea of an extensive scouting and free-agent sign-ings from the Los Angeles Rams where he worked as the team's publicity director. In the mid-1950s, the Rams had the first paid scouts in the NFL. Rams owner Dan Reeves (no relation to the former Cowboy running back who now coaches the Denver Broncos) paid some college coaches $500 a year to spot talent for him. Reeves also gave assistants $50 a year for the same purpose. The Rams sent out questionnaires to dozens of small colleges to get information about prospects. Dallas didn't invent the system, they borrowed it.

MYTH: *The Cowboys coaching staff is one of the best in the NFL.*
FACT: Then why do the current crop of Cowboys as-sistants have a combined head coaching record of 145–224–11? Landry was a head coach for two years before he won a game. And the five former head coaches on the staff all have losing records: Neill Armstrong was 30–34 with the Chicago Bears before he got fired; Dick Nolan, an old Landry crony from their New York Giant days, was 70–85–5 as a head coach with the 49ers and Saints; Jim Shofner was 2–31 with TCU, recently one of the worst college teams in the nation; Gene Stallings went 27–45–1 with Texas A&M before the Aggies fired him; Jim Meyers was 4–5–1 at Iowa State and 12–24–4 at Texas A&M; and former Landry assistants Dan Reeves, Mike Ditka and John Mackovic haven't done much better. Reeves has led the Broncos to a 21–21 record, including a 1983 playoff disaster against the Seattle Seahawks; Ditka has an

11–14 record with the Bears; Mackovic led the Chiefs to a 6–10 record in his first season at the helm. Not exactly the stuff that coaching legends are made of.

MYTH: *The Cowboys' fans are the greatest in the world.*
FACT: Only 43,521 Cowboys loyalists showed up to see their heroes lose a 1983 playoff game against the Los Angeles Rams. It was the smallest crowd in the history of Texas Stadium. 20,015 no-shows. The TV viewers in Dallas were able to see the game only be-

The Cowboys faithful—even when they show up, they wish they hadn't. ▼

15

cause two Dallas businessmen bought the last 3,500 tickets in order to lift the TV blackout. Ever hear of a team not selling out for a playoff game? The Washington Redskins have sold out every home game since 1966—that's 132 in a row through 1983—including many, many years when they weren't doing nearly as well as the Cowboys. The best description for Cowboys fans is fair-weather front-runners.

MYTH: *The Cowboys stand for the American way of life.*
FACT: Unless, of course, you think America includes Democrats and unions. Tom Landry joined Republican John Connolly's presidential advisory team in 1979 and later endorsed Ronald Reagan. (Let's hope he didn't advise Reagan on how to defend against the bomb.) He also did commercials for right-wing Senator Jesse Helms of North Carolina in 1979. And during the 1982 dispute between the NFL and the NFL Players Association, the Cowboys promised six of their players raises of as much as 400 percent. Three of the six canceled a trip to a union meeting. Some pro-union advocates on the Cowboys roster accused management of trying to undermine the union. Quarterback Danny White criticized the NFLPA for threatening to strike, a move that endeared him to management, but not to his teammates.

MYTH: *The Cowboys take care of their fans.*
FACT: When the Cowboys opened Texas Stadium in 1971, they made the fans pay for it. Up front. To get a season ticket between the 30-yard lines, fans had to

Would Landry let the President call his own plays? Only Rolaids Roger knows for sure. ▶

purchase a $1,000 stadium bond, a $63 season ticket, and a $20 season parking pass. They also had to agree to buy that season ticket for the next 32 years or lose their option on it. Owner Clint Murchison told *Esquire* in 1972 that he thought the Cowboys had lost a whole group of season ticket holders in the $12,000–$20,000-a-year income range who couldn't afford Texas Stadium season tickets because of the high-priced bonds. "If we discriminated against them, we discriminated against them," he said. "But no more than all America discriminates against people who don't have enough money to buy everything they want." But for football fans with big bucks and for corporations looking for a tax write-off, the Cowboys not only have season tickets, they have private boxes that sold in 1971 at $50,000 a pop. Add to that a private club where the only liquor in the whole stadium is sold. Irving, Texas is dry, but the state legislature passed a bill allowing liquor-by-the-drink at stadiums and airports in dry areas if approved by local officials. Naturally, the Irving city fathers voted to make the luxurious suites at Texas Stadium and the exclusive Stadium Club wet. But until recently, the fans in the stands couldn't buy beer.

MYTH: *Dallas is America's team.*
FACT: You better have someone read this book to you v-e-r-y s-l-o-w-l-y.

3

Great Lowlights in Cowboys History

Are you tired of gloating Cowboys fans bragging about two Super Bowl victories and other meaningless wins? Well, remind them that it ain't always the Cowboys who finish on top. Here are some of the great games that Cowboys Haters relish and the Dallas Corporates would rather forget.

A Great Beginning

August 6, 1960—In their first game ever, a pre-season contest in Seattle, the Cowboys lost to the San Francisco 49ers, 16–10.

Dallas Debut

August 19, 1960—The fledgling Cowboys gave the hometown fans a glimpse of the disappointment to

come. The 'Pokes held a 10–7 lead over the world champion Baltimore Colts with less than a minute to play. But Johnny Unitas calmly tossed a 62-yard touchdown to Lenny Moore and the Colts trotted away with a 14–10 win.

First Official NFL Loss

September 24, 1960—In the Cowboys' first regular-season NFL game, Bobby Layne led a fourth-quarter Pittsburgh rally to secure a 35–28 Steelers victory, the first of many, many Steeler wins over the Cowboys.

Penalty Points

September 23, 1962—For the first time in memory, points were awarded for a penalty in an NFL game. The

Cowboys were detected holding in the end zone on a 99-yard touchdown pass from Eddie LeBaron to Frank Clarke. The Steelers got a safety and eventually won the game 30–28.

★ GREAT PLAYS, MEMORABLE MOMENTS ★

In 1962, Tex Schramm asked the Service Bureau Corporation, then a subsidiary of IBM, to help "America's Team" develop a computerized scouting system. SBC sent over Salam Querishi, a native of India, who knew a lot about bits and bytes but little about football. That was the beginning of the Computerized Cowboys.

Kicked by Colts

January 15, 1966—In their first appearance in post-season play, the Cowboys began their proud tradition of losing playoff games. That first loss was a 35–3 drubbing by the Baltimore Colts in the now-defunct Playoff Bowl in Miami. The Colts' starting and backup quarterbacks, Johnny Unitas and Gary Cuozzo, were injured and could not play. So in came halfback-turned-quarterback Tom Matte. With the plays taped to his wrist, Matte had little trouble in swamping the Wowboys. Just think what the score would have been if Unitas had been healthy.

Baker Boots Old Mates

November 6, 1966—Former Cowboy kicker Sam Baker booted the winning field goal in a 24–23 contest against the Philadelphia Eagles. The Dallas special teams had a great afternoon, giving up kickoff returns of 93 and 90 yards for touchdowns by Timmy Brown and a 67-yard punt return for a TD by Aaron Martin.

New Year, Old Results

January 1, 1967—Bart Starr passed for four touchdowns before a disheartened Cotton Bowl crowd as Green Bay whipped Dallas 34–27 for the NFL championship. A last-minute Cowboys threat was thwarted when Packer safety Tom Brown intercepted Don Meredith's fourth-down pass in the end zone. Dallas received—and deserved—a reputation for choking in the big ones.

The image of Bart Starr (15) diving for the winning touchdown will be forever frozen in the minds of Cowboys haters. (AP/Wide World Photos)▼

Ice Bowl Beauty

December 31, 1967—In one of football's most memorable games, Green Bay won the NFL title by outlasting the Cowboys 21–17 in the famous Ice Bowl. Bart Starr sneaked into the end zone behind guard Jerry Kramer and center Ken Bowman with only 13 seconds left in the game for the winning TD. The frozen Green Bay linemen cleared a path for Starr by rubbing defensive tackle Jethro Pugh's face in the snow. The Sissies from Texas couldn't handle the 13-below-zero temperature nor the Packers offensive line. Moral of this game: Real men don't wear Silver and Blue.

Buried by Browns

December 21, 1968—On the shores of beautiful Lake Erie sits Cleveland's Municipal Stadium. On this day, it became a Cowboys tomb. Cleveland quarterback Bill Nelsen and running back Leroy Kelly led the Browns to the NFL Eastern Conference title by beating Dallas 31–20. The Cowboys made it easy by giving up 21 points in less than four minutes. Nelsen threw for two scores and Kelly ran for two more. Cleveland gave Don Meredith the game ball for throwing back-to-back interceptions that led to touchdowns.

Cleveland: Take Two

December 28, 1969—For the second straight year, Dallas and Cleveland met for the Eastern Conference title, this time on Texas soil. Dallas used the home field to its advantage and held the Browns to only 38 points. The Cowboys, behind Craig Morton, managed 14. Morton's passing prowess led to an 88-yard interception return for a Cleveland touchdown, and the Browns got some unexpected points when a punt hit Cowboy tackle Rayfield Wright on the leg, Cleveland recovered, and added another six.

Gabriel's Horn

January 3, 1970—After losing the Eastern Conference title again, the Cowboys advanced to the meaningless Playoff Bowl. (Vince Lombardi called it the "Loser's Bowl.") This time, Dallas met Los Angeles, and Ram quarterback Roman Gabriel threw four heavenly touchdown passes against the Dallasites. Ram receiver Jack Snow scored on pass plays covering 67 and 49 yards. Meanwhile, Dallas quarterback Craig Morton was throwing two interceptions and leading the Cowboys to 87 total passing yards. Final score: Los Angeles 31, Dallas zip.

Minnesota Rout

October 18, 1970—The Vikings' Purple People Eaters—Carl Eller, Alan Page, Jim Marshall, and Gary Larsen—feasted during a 54–13 Minnesota win. Viking Ed Sharockman scored a TD on a 23-yard return of a blocked punt and another on a 34-yard interception return. Dallas quarterback Craig Morton threw one interception and understudy Roger Staubach showed he was paying attention by throwing three of his own. Minnesota's 54 points stands as a single-game record against the vaunted Dallas defense.

Monday Night Bust

November 16, 1970—The Cowboys were a monumental flop on their *Monday Night Football* debut. The St. Louis Cardinals gave the Cowboys a 38–0 lesson in humility before a national TV audience and a Dallas crowd. When Cowboy quarterback Craig Morton threw his third interception of the night, the Cowboys faithful began chanting, "We Want Meredith! We Want Meredith!" Dandy Don heard the chants from his perch in the ABC-TV booth alongside Howard Cosell and Keith Jackson. On the air, Meredith said there was no way he wanted to be a part of the humiliation taking place on the field below. Just two seasons earlier, the Dallas crowd had booed Meredith unmercifully.

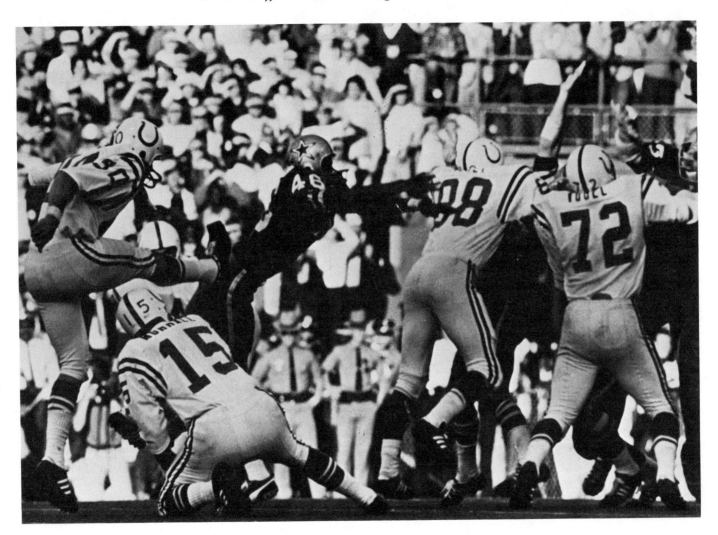

Baltimore's Jim O'Brien left the Colts a leg up in Super Bowl V with this 32-yarder. ◀

Super Loss I

January 17, 1971—The Cowboys finally made it to the Super Bowl, but Cowboys haters were not disappointed as Craig Morton threw three interceptions and Duane Thomas fumbled on the Colts two-yard line to kill a scoring opportunity. Baltimore, led by aging Earl Morrall, won 16–13 when Jim O'Brien kicked a 32-yard field goal with only five seconds remaining in Super Bowl V. The Can't-Win-The-Big-One Legend grew.

★ GREAT PLAYS, MEMORABLE MOMENTS ★

Ball control offense at its best: Cowboy punter Ron Widby set a Super Bowl record against Baltimore in 1971 for most punts in a game (nine).

By George!

December 31, 1972—The Redskins hailed in the New Year by kicking the Cowboys all the way back to Dallas. By the time George Allen's "Over-The-Hill Gang" had finished with the Corporates, the scoreboard read Washington 26, Dallas 3. Billy Kilmer, the Redskins' pudgy quarterback, completed 14 of 18 passes for 194 yards. All-Pro receiver Charley Taylor caught seven passes for 146 yards and Redskin kicker Curt Knight connected on four field goals, a championship game record.

Corralled in D.C.

October 8, 1973—The Redskins took a 14–7 lead over the Cowboys before a frenzied crowd of Cowboys Haters on a Monday night in Washington. In a last-gasp effort to snatch victory, Dallas quarterback Roger Staubach passed to snuff-dippin' Walt Garrison (one of the few *real* cowboys to ever play for Dallas). The Dodge Ram-tough Garrison caught the ball inches from the goal line only to have skinny little Redskin safety Ken Houston lower the boom with a bruising tackle that stopped the Cowpoke short of paydirt with 38 seconds to play. Washington won again.

Walt Garrison learned this takedown hold from Kenny Houston on national TV. (AP/Wide World Photos) ▼

Vikes Spike Dallas

December 30, 1973—The Cowboys stayed on a downhill roll in championship encounters. This time the Minnesota Vikings did the honors. Fran Tarkenton's 54-yard touchdown pass to John Gilliam and Bobby Bryant's 63-yard interception return for another TD gave the Vikes a 27–10 victory. Dallas fans suggested that a hangman's noose be part of the team's official uniform. Red Cross volunteers offered to teach coaches the proper first-aid techniques for choking.

RFK Redux

November 2, 1975—Washington's Ken Houston (again!) stole a Roger Staubach pass and Billy Kilmer scored the winning touchdown in overtime as the Redskins whipped the Cowboys 30–24. The Texas congressional delegation urged Congress to pass a resolution banning further Cowboy embarrassments, but it failed by a vote of 412–23.

Super Loss II

January 18, 1976—Terry Bradshaw started a trend in leading the Steelers to a 27–21 victory over the Cowboys in Super Bowl X. America slept safer that night with the knowledge that Cowboy quarterback Roger Staubach, a Naval Academy graduate, was no longer guarding our shores. Staubach had tossed three interceptions. Reggie Harrison of the Steelers blocked a Mitch (Who?) Hoopes punt for a safety, and Leapin' Lynn Swann spent the afternoon dancing past cornerback Mark Washington for four catches and 161

The Dallas kicking game played right into the hands of the Steelers in Super Bowl X. Pittsburgh's Reggie Harrison, not the Cowboys' line, did the blocking. ▲

yards. Swann's coup de grace was a 64-yard TD reception. Cowboys fans left the game muttering, "Choke, choke, choke."

Super Loss III

January 21, 1979—Super Bowl XIII marked the first time in NFL history that two teams met in a super rematch. And history repeated itself. Terry Bradshaw proved he wasn't as dumb as everyone in Texas thought by setting a Super Bowl record with 318 yards passing. It took Dallas cornerback Benny Barnes four quarters to figure out a way to stop Lynn Swann—he tripped him and got penalized 33 yards. Two plays later, Franco Harris barged across the goal line for six. The Cowboys saw their hopes for a victory slip through the fingers of tight end Jackie Smith, who dropped a Staubach pass in the end zone. For the second time in three years, the Steelers left Dallas on the short end of the championship game. Again, the margin was four points, 35–31.

★ GREAT PLAYS, MEMORABLE MOMENTS ★

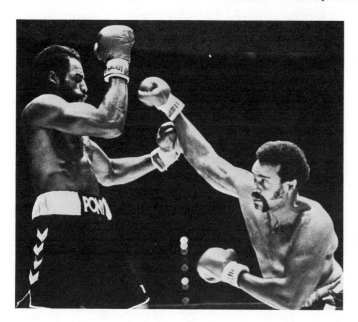

John Wayne the cowboy would never pick on someone smaller and physically inferior. Not so the Cowboys of Dallas. Ed "Too Tall" Jones left the Cowboys in 1979 to pursue a career as a professional boxer. In his most memorable fight, the 6'9" defensive end picked on 6'1" Jesus "Yaqui" Meneses. The mismatch was staged in Las Cruces, New Mexico, before a national television audience. Jones won a decision, but not before the crowd booed and laughed when Meneses pushed Too Tall to the canvas in the sixth round and then hit the fallen Cowboy when he was down. Jones also distinguished himself in the ring by fracturing both hands and breaking a foot during his one-year career.

"Floats like a stork,"/They said of Too Tall;/"He can put on the gloves/But he can't box at all." ◄

Rammed at Home

December 30, 1979—A stunned Texas Stadium crowd watched Dallas' hopes for a second consecutive Super Bowl berth disappear through the hole in the roof. Los Angeles rammed the 'Pokes 21–19 for the NFC title. The highlight of the game came when "Rolaids Roger" Staubach threw the last pass of his NFL career to offensive guard Herb Scott. Hey, at least Scott caught it.

Philly Finale

January 11, 1981—Wilbert Montgomery, a Texas lad, rushed for 194 yards through a porous Cowboys defense as the Philadelphia Eagles dumped Dallas 20–7 in the NFC championship game. The mighty Dallas ground game screeched to a halt as Tony Dorsett could only wiggle for 41 yards and the entire Dallas offense managed a meager 90 yards rushing. Danny White, the newest Cowboy quarterback, performed miserably, with only 12 pass completions in 31 tries. Dallas mascot Crazy Ray got a little crazier.

Cable-Car Classic

January 9, 1982—Joe Montana passed six yards to wide receiver Dwight Clark, whose stretching catch in the end zone gave the 49ers a 28–27 victory over "America's Team." The Montana-to-Clark heroics came with 51 seconds left to play and spelled defeat for the Cowboys in their third straight NFC championship game. Dallas quarterback Danny White faced the same question from Cowboys fans as did his predecessors—can he win the big one? Obviously not.

Turn Out the Lights

January 22, 1983—Washington's Dexter Manley, a Texas native who wisely plays football out of the state, knocked Danny White unconscious just before the end of the first half in the NFC title game at RFK Stadium. White's understudy, Gary Hogeboom, tossed a pair of touchdown passes in the second half to make the game exciting. But Manley capped a brilliant day by batting a Hogeboom pass into the waiting hands of teammate Darryl Grant, who lumbered into the end zone to clinch a 31–27 Washington victory. Clint Murchison ordered a new computer.

No! No! No!

December 11, 1983—Not all chokes have to come in the playoffs. In the biggest game of the year, the Cowboys had fourth down and inches at the Redskins' 49-yard line. Danny White attempted to draw the Redskins offsides. But Washington didn't bite, and as Tom Landry screamed on the sidelines, Dallas ran a play and lost two yards. Washington scalped 'em 31–10. "Don't think we're not human out there," Landry declared after the game. We noticed, Tom, we noticed.

A White Christmas

December 26, 1983—Cowboys haters will long dream of a (Danny) White Christmas. In fact, the final three weeks of the 1983 season were a little bit of heaven. The Cowboys ended '83 with three consecutive losses by a combined score of 97–44. The Los Angeles Rams put the trimming on the Christmas tree

AND THE SURVEY SAYS . . .

The producers of the television game show *Family Feud* thought they had a winner in 1980 when they invited members of the Dallas Cowboys and the Dallas Cowboys Cheerleaders to appear on the show.

Host Richard Dawson asked Harvey Martin, Danny White, Tony Dorsett, Charlie Waters, and Larry Cole a series of questions about everyday topics. Members of "America's Team" gave some answers that did little to destroy the notion that most football players are a few bricks shy of a load.

Consider these exchanges:

Dawson: What invention of the 20th century are you most thankful for? (Remember, the Cowboys are playing the Cheerleaders.)

Martin: Since this is women, 20th century, I'll say bra.

Dawson: Name something men do when they nick themselves shaving.

Dorsett: Aftershave.

Dawson: Name something that's hard to learn how to ride.

Martin: Spanish. (That didn't get on the air.)

Dawson: Name someone whose approval you want.

Waters: God. It's either that (sic) or Coach Landry.

Dawson: Name something an airplane needs to fly.

Cole: Air.

Dawson: Name a vegetable people stuff.

Cole: Watermelon.

With such a display of intellect, is it surprising that the following joke made its way into Cowboys haters' hearts?

In Dallas, what do they call a combined I.Q. of 40?
Dee-fense. Dee-fense.

Harvey Martin:
Feud for thought ▶

by whipping the Corporates 24–17 in the NFC wildcard game before a chilled Texas Stadium crowd. The great Dallas "fans" stayed away in droves, with 20,015 no-shows. Those who attended watched Danny White throw three interceptions, one of which was returned an NFC playoff record 94 yards by Ram LeRoy Irvin. Cowboys President Tex Schramm summed the game up nicely: "It will be just like the late 1960s all over again. Everyone will write we can't win the big one."

Yup.

The Organization

"Mr. Murchison runs this as a business, kind of like you'd run General Motors." —*Gil Brandt*

Truer words were never spoken. "America's Team" is, first and foremost, a business. When the Cowboys' brass mentions the bottom line, they're not talking about the Cheerleaders.

Like most successful corporations, the Cowboys have a strict sense of organization. And the Corporate Cowboys' roots of success can be traced initially to a fellow named George Halas.

The patriarch of the Chicago Bears took more than a passing interest in the fledgling Cowboys. In fact, Papa Bear was so involved in the early days of the franchise that a Washington sports columnist referred to the Texas team in 1962 as the "Halas Cowboys."

The late, great Halas was chairman of the NFL expansion committee and was instrumental in persuading the other NFL owners to put a team in Dallas. After accomplishing that feat, Halas was determined to make the Cowboys a success. The upstart American Football League was just starting in 1960 and AFL founder Lamar Hunt had staked out Dallas as one of the early battle sites for the professional football dollar.

Halas suggested to Murchison that he hire "a young fellow with CBS Sports who has a good head for football" named Tex Schramm.

Murchison was quick to follow up and the organization began to take shape around a California-born former sportswriter named Tex; a Wisconsin baby photographer named Gil Brandt; a strait-laced coach named Landry; and an owner who was once a strapping 5'7", 130-pound halfback at the Massachusetts Institute of Technology.

But if Murchison was shallow in the stature department, he was certainly deep enough where it counted most: his pockets. The oilman shelled out $600,000

for the franchise in 1960 and turned the operation over to Tex Schramm.

And Schramm found himself on the receiving end of yet another George Halas favor. Papa Bear understood the value of hometown publicity and felt the Cowboys should have the rights to SMU star Don Meredith. But Dallas was not allowed to draft college players in 1960,

Landry, Schramm, and Brandt cut deals that would make J. R. Ewing proud. ▲

so Halas drafted Meredith in the third round—even though the Cowboys had already signed Dandy to a personal services contract. Halas didn't care. He traded the flashy quarterback to Dallas for a third-round pick in the 1962 draft.

After Papa Bear's death in 1983, Murchison told a Dallas sportswriter that Halas had once called him during a college all-star game in which Meredith was spectacular.

"How do you like *our* quarterback?" Halas asked.

"Our" quarterback gave Tex Schramm a player he could promote. And make no mistake, sports fans: promotion is the name of Schramm's game. To Tex Schramm, a Cowboys fan is born every minute.

With Murchison giving his general manager free rein, Tex Schramm applied the finer points of marketing and press agentry to the Cowboys franchise. With his background as a sportswriter, publicity director and general manager for the Los Angeles Rams and as CBS sports executive, he was ideally suited for the task at hand.

But Schramm's most formidable weapon might just be his association with a fellow by the name of Pete Rozelle.

Schramm hired Rozelle as the Rams' publicity director when Tex was the team's general manager. When Tex moved on to greener pastures at CBS, Rozelle was elevated to the general manager's post. And when Tex was putting the Cowboys together, guess who was named NFL commissioner?

Not that the Cowboys get preferential treatment by

Young Dandy Don Meredith shouldered the responsibilities of being the Cowboys' shining star, before a horrendous offensive line and plays from the sidelines took their toll. ▲

31

California-born Tex Schramm thinks a Cowboys fan is born every minute. ▲

the NFL, mind you, but Schramm's thirty-year-plus relationship with the commissioner doesn't hurt. Al Davis of Oakland/LA Raider fame put the situation in perspective for *Sports Illustrated* last year.

"The Cowboys are wired to the league office, everyone knows that," said Davis. "And you can bet every game official knows that, too. If there's one team that's going to get a break, it's Dallas—on the calls, on the scheduling, on the Competition Committee, on everything else relating to league matters."

Rozelle would have plenty of reasons to grant the Cowboys president any wish.

In 1966, for example, Rozelle made headlines by surprising the sports world with the announcement of the AFL-NFL merger. Schramm and Lamar Hunt had been holding secret negotiations months before, but it was Rozelle who was allowed to stand in the limelight.

And when the Oakland/Los Angeles Raiders took the NFL to court, Schramm was with Rozelle throughout the five-week trial. (No wonder Al Davis cares so little for Rozelle, Schramm or the Cowboys.)

Add to all of the above the fact that Schramm chairs the NFL's competition committee and you have all the ingredients for home cooking, Cowboys style.

Schramm used more than just personal friendships to make the Cowboys a corporate wonder. Tex would kill for national television exposure. He "volunteered" the Cowboys for games on any night of the week. Want a Thanksgiving Day winner? Put on the Cowboys. Need a Monday night season opener? Take my Cowboys. Want to televise nationally from the North Pole on

★ GREAT PLAYS, MEMORABLE MOMENTS ★

The Dallas Cowboys team display at the Pro Football Hall of Fame in Canton, Ohio, is one of the smallest in the shrine. It consists of an old Bob Lilly jersey.

Ironically, Lilly's jersey hangs next to the Washington Redskins display. Lilly, by the way, is the only real Cowboy in the Hall of Fame. Three former Cowboys are enshrined in Canton—Herb Adderly, Forrest Gregg, and Lance Alworth—but that talented trio played the bulk of their careers in Green Bay, Green Bay and San Diego, respectively. Cowboys assistant coach Ernie Stautner is also in the Hall of Fame for his heroics as a Pittsburgh Steeler defensive lineman.

Christmas Eve? You got it.

Thus, the Cowboys and big-time pro football TV ratings grew up together.

"The Cowboys came along just as television was really improving its coverage of the NFL," remembers Pete Gent, the erstwhile Cowboy. "Pro football was really becoming America's sport and the Cowboys emerged as the expansion team out of Texas who a lot of unattached fans, with no team to pull for, started to follow. The Cowboys knew how to merchandise. They knew how to take a product and make it valuable."

Valuable is right. The Cowboys outsell their nearest NFL Properties rival, the Steelers, by almost a two-to-

Clint Murchison had the last laugh, selling "America's Team" to an Aggie named Bum for a Texas-sized profit. ▲

one margin. There's gold in them thar T-shirts, posters, playing cards and coffee mugs, padnuh. And Tex Schramm realized it and made sure that the Cowboys got a Texas-sized share.

Schramm came up with the idea for *The Dallas Cowboys Official Weekly*, a nifty little newspaper with a circulation of more than 100,000 throughout the U.S. and even in some foreign countries. For $15.95 a year, Cowboys crazies can subscribe to the official team propaganda sheet.

And let's not forget radio. Schramm sure didn't. The Cowboys have the largest radio network in the NFL, naturally. The Dallas Cowboys Network covers Texas and 14 other states ranging from Tennessee to Hawaii. That's 167 stations broadcasting Dallas fumbles in English. Eleven more stations air a Spanish version in Texas, Mexico, and Florida. The Cowboys radio saturation would have been extended in 1983 if the federal government hadn't blocked an attempt by CBS (who else?) to buy the Cowboys' flagship station in Dallas and the entire network.

Newspapers. Television. Radio. Schramm didn't miss a beat. Or a boob. Who do you think came up with the idea to put sex on the sidelines in the form of the Dallas Cowboys Cheerleaders? Mr. Schramm, take a bow.

But just how successful have Schramm's efforts been? Well, a nationwide Gallup Poll taken in November 1983 gave us a hint. Respondents were asked what they associated with Dallas. Eleven percent said the TV show *Dallas*. That was third place in the final standing. Seventeen percent said the assassination of President John F. Kennedy. Second place.

Twenty-eight percent said the Dallas Cowboys.

Image is a top priority with the Corporates. In 1983, Dallas hired a former FBI agent to be the team security director. Schramm said Larry Wansley was hired to help players stay out of personal trouble, namely drugs and gambling.

One of Wansley's first acts was to turn the Cowboys training camp into what Dallas sportswriters called "Fort Landry." The Cowboy training camp in Thousand Oaks, California, was dotted with barricades, checkpoints, and 24-hour security patrols.

No one escaped.

You can imagine what the security will be like at the Corporates new headquarters outside Dallas. The Cowboy Taj Mahal will include three football fields, a lecture hall, a spa complete with a eucalyptus room, and a locker room and studio for the cheerleaders.

But the news that rocked Big D in 1983 wasn't over the new headquarters or Fort Landry.

The Cowboys are for sale. Clint Murchison, Jr., announced plans to sell "America's Team."

A combination of health problems for the 58-year-old Murchison and a desire to sort out the tangled estate of brother John resulted in the public announcement by Tex Schramm that the Cowboys would begin screening potential buyers.

Don't feel too sorry for Clint, though. He sold "America's Team" and the remaining sixty-five years on the lease of the stadium with the hole in the roof for $80 million. Not a bad return on a $600,000 investment.

For Cowboys haters, the selling of "America's Team"

had all the makings of a silver cloud with a dark lining. Schramm carefully screened potential buyers and made sure that one Texas E. Schramm retained real control over the franchise. That's right: the new owners of the Cowboys agreed to pay $60 million for the franchise and at the same time agreed to leave Schramm in control. And the principal owner coughed up another $20 million for rights to the Texas Stadium lease. Sound bizarre? It gets better.

"America's Team" is now owned by a Texas Aggie.

Harvey Roberts Bright, a 1943 graduate of Texas A&M who answers to the nickname "Bum," is the man who took the Cowboys off Murchison's hands by promising to keep his nose out of Tex Schramm's business. Just like he kept his nose out of the Aggies football coaching situation. With the A&M president publicly backing coach Tom Wilson, Board of Regents Chairman Bum Bright maneuvered behind the scenes and arranged for Wilson's firing and the hiring of Jackie Sherrill. Money was no problem in that deal, either. Sherrill became the Aggie head coach and the first million-dollar college football coach in America.

And that's no Aggie joke.

This is also the same Bum Bright who is fond of saying that unless a boy goes to Texas A&M, he's off to a wrong start; sorts his pocket money in sequential order by Federal Reserve Bank district number; and is ranked by *Forbes* as one of the 400 wealthiest men in America, with a personal worth of about $125 million.

Bum is also a man of compassion. He allowed his bride-to-be, who just happened to be his secretary at the time, to leave work at 4 P.M. for their 6 P.M. wedding.

And when it comes to politics, Bum can match his record against any arch-conservative Republican, including Tom Landry. Bum was one of three Dallas businessmen who helped pay for a controversial newspaper ad written by John Birch Society members. The ad asked why the then-President of the United States had allowed subordinates to "go soft on Communists," and other niceties.

It ran in *The Dallas Morning News* on November 22, 1963, under the heading, "Welcome Mr. Kennedy to Dallas."

"America's Team" has a new owner. Gig 'em, Aggies.

Bum Bright, the pride of the Aggies, with his newest toy ▶

THE OATH OF HYPOCRISY

One way to judge a pro football franchise is by the way it takes care of its injured players. After all, football is a business, and players represent the raw materials, the machinery, the inventory. You can't play and you certainly can't win if the machinery isn't kept in tip-top shape.

But while the Cowboys pride themselves on their year-round training program, first-class workout facilities, and modern equipment, some present and former Cowboys argue that management's attitude toward injured players has more to do with the bottom line than with the well-being of the individual. When you're healthy and producing, you're a valuable individual. When you're hurt and sitting on the sidelines, you're a debit, not a credit.

Take the case of the Cowboy place-kicker Rafael Septien, who played much of the 1982 season with what the Cowboys told him was a "pulled groin." Painful, but playable. Once the season ended, the Cowboys informed Rafael that he needed surgery to repair a hernia. Oh, he had had a hernia all along. The Cowboys just neglected to tell him about it.

Outrageous? Not according to the Book of Landry.

"You tell him [Septien] and he worries,"

Landry told a Dallas newspaper when it was revealed that the Cowboys had withheld medical information from their kicker. "And he doesn't kick well. We just didn't tell him."

And he doesn't kick well???

When a Dallas newspaper used the Septien case as a reason to examine the way the Cowboys treat their broken machinery, the results were surprising. Present and former members of "America's Team" criticized the Cowboys for not having a suitable rehabilitation program, misdiagnosing injuries, and withholding medical information. Some players were outraged by the Septien case. Others were not surprised.

And what about the Cowboys management?

"No, it wasn't an embarrassment," said team president Tex Schramm.

One player, who asked the paper not to use his name, said: "The way I see it, I feel like if you got hurt, the Cowboys feel you screwed up. They write you off. They just feel that no matter who it is, there's always another body to take his place."

And he doesn't kick well???

Fullback Robert Newhouse, a 12-year Cowboy veteran, suffered a leg injury in the 1979 season

Gil Brandt:
You say it's broken?
Well, give him two
aspirin and hide
the x-rays.◀

opener. Three weeks later, his injury was diagnosed as a broken leg. When a Dallas newspaper writing about the Cowboys medical practices asked Cowboys Vice President Gil Brandt about the Newhouse injury, Brandt said he didn't remember Newhouse ever being hurt.

Brandt should read the Cowboys media guide. Newhouse's biography said a stress fracture in his lower left leg slowed him in the 1979 season.

And he doesn't kick well???

In 1982, linebacker Anthony Dickerson suffered an injury that was diagnosed as a pulled groin. Those groin pulls are tricky in Dallas. Dickerson's injury turned out to be a separation of the pelvis.

And he doesn't kick well???

In 1963, rookie tight end Pettis Norman was examined by the Cowboys team doctor. Norman wasn't told he had 25 percent disability in each knee. Norman learned about it years later when he was suing a San Diego doctor for malpractice. Norman's suit against the Cowboys was thrown out of court.

And he doesn't kick well???

Mike Gaechter, a former safety; Leon Donohue, a former guard; and Willie Townes, a former defensive end, all filed $1 million lawsuits against the Cowboys claiming mistreatment of injuries. Their lawyer is trying to get them back on the court docket.

Richard Grimmett, who played for the Cowboys in 1979, won $24,000 in 1983 on an out-of-court settlement on a workman's compensation suit he filed. But such victories are rare. Offensive lineman Norm Wells spent the 1981 season on injured reserve due to a knee injury. He filed a workman's compensation suit against the Cowboys in 1982, but later told his attorney to drop the suit.

Lawsuits do not amuse the Cowboys. Wells told his attorney the Cowboys asked him to turn in his playbook if he filed suit. He got paid for the 1981 season, but is no longer with the team.

And look at what happened to Pettis Norman after he filed suit: the Cowboys took his name off their Christmas card list.

Tom Blandry, T. O. C. T. D. C. H. E. H.

The man who personifies the Dallas Cowboys is NOT Rolaids Roger Staubach or Dandy Don Meredith or not-so-Dandy Danny White. It's the man who walks the sidelines. The Old Bomber Pilot. The NFL's only living Neiman-Marcus mannequin.

So return with us to those thrilling days of yesteryear as we relive the best-forgotten moments of Tom Blandry, The Only Coach The Dallas Cowboys Have Ever Had.

For openers, he began his pro football career as a Yankee. He signed with the New York Yankees of the All-American Football Conference in 1949. A year later, he moved over to the New York Giants when the NFL and All-American Football Conference merged.

But before the merger, Landry became part of AAFC history. On November 20, 1949, Cleveland quarterback Otto Graham and wide receiver Mac Speedie combined to set an AAFC record with 11 receptions and 228 yards. Guess who played cornerback for the Yankees in that 31–0 debacle? And guess whom Cleveland coach Paul Brown accused of taking a cheap shot at his star quarterback?

On September 29, 1952, in the first NFL game on Texas soil, the Dallas Texans lost to the New York Giants, 24–6. The Cotton Bowl crowd got a glimpse of Landry under pressure. The Giants' defensive back

38

distinguished himself by fumbling a punt, which the Texans recovered.

Nineteen fifty-two just wasn't Landry's year. During a game against Pittsburgh, the Giants lost their starting and backup quarterbacks. In came Landry, who had played some quarterback at the University of Texas (at Austin).

The Giants lost 63–7 and Landry would never play quarterback again in the NFL. During that game, Pittsburgh defensive tackle Ernie Stautner got to the quarterback in a big way. Stautner put his fist in Landry's face, breaking Landry's nose. Stautner is still paying for the misdeed: he's one of Landry's assistant coaches.

Landry retired as a player in 1955 and became a full-time assistant coach for the Giants along with a fellow named Vince Lombardi. While Landry was a player, the Giants never won an NFL title. In 1956, Landry's revolutionary 4–3 defense, anchored by middle linebacker Sam Huff, staked the Giants to their last NFL title and set the stage for what historians feel was the greatest game in NFL history.

More than any other single game, the 1958 NFL title match between the Giants and the Colts ranks as the one event that put pro football on the map. The Giants would have won that classic duel if they could have stopped the passes from Johnny Unitas to Raymond Berry. Despite Landry's double-teaming defense, the Unitas-to-Berry combination clicked when it had to. The national TV audience and the more than 64,000 stunned fans in Yankee Stadium watched as the Colts came back in the closing seconds to tie the game and send the contest into overtime. Once in overtime, Unitas and Berry set up the game-winning run by Alan Ameche. Colts 23, Giants 17. Tom Landry had lost his first big test as a pro coach.

★ GREAT PLAYS, MEMORABLE MOMENTS ★

Of the many Dallas weaknesses, pass defense may be the weakest. In 1976, Steeler Lynn Swann set a Super Bowl record for most yards gained receiving. Dallas held Swann to 161 yards.

Upon leaving the Giants, Landry jumped from the frying pan into the fire. He joined the expansion Dallas Rangers (later changed to Cowboys) in 1959 and began his first "Five-Year Plan." The five-year plan was a flop. Landry's five-year record: 13–46–4. Dallas fans were calling for his scalp (or a reasonable facsimile thereof) after his fourth straight losing season in 1963. Instead, owner Clint Murchison gave him an unheard-of ten-year contract. Landry thanked him by going 5–8–1 in 1964.

★ ★ ★

Nineteen sixty-four will long be remembered as the year the Cowboys welcomed one Pete Gent to their fold. Gent just did not fit Landry's mold. The two men had a communication problem.

Once, Landry decided to move Gent from split end to flanker for a game against Philadelphia. Landry told Gent: "You're going to play on the other side next week."

Gent responded: "I'm going to play for Philadelphia?"

★ ★ ★

Landry has won many awards and honors for his efforts on and off the football field: The Order of the Leather Helmet for distinguished service to football; Man of the Year in 1981 by the *Football News*; the Horatio Alger Award in 1983 for his inspirational rise to prominence.

But for Cowboys haters, two awards are most memorable. One was his being named one of America's best-dressed men in 1976 for "his choice of attractive hats and personal clothes coordination." The Cowboys lost to the Rams in the first round of the playoffs that year.

And the second award involved his off-the-field efforts on behalf of morality in Dallas. The prosecuting

A man of many moods:

Elation

Anger

Enthusiasm

Despair

attorney in an obscenity case called Landry to the stand as an "expert witness." The man with an autographed picture of Billy Graham in his office watched the film in question and said, yes, it was obscene. (The film in question was *not* the famed 1967 Dallas–Green Bay Ice Bowl game film.)

For his pious efforts, Landry was named *Hustler's* "Asshole of the Month."

Fueled by his courtroom victory over smut, Landry moved in 1983 to ban individualism on his football team. Specifically, players would not be allowed to "spike" the ball after a touchdown for fear of a stiff fine.

Wide receiver Butch Johnson, whose "California Quake" end zone dance had become a crowd favorite, complained about the new rule but never broke it.

Don't look for Mr. Morality to back the Equal Rights Amendment, either. In a 1983 interview, Alicia Landry, The Only Wife Tom Landry Has Ever Had, explained the couple's approach to golf:

He got tired of waiting on me to get to the green because I take so long. So he plays both balls off the tee. He'll just go to the one that is farthest out and work it to the green. Then I'll putt.

Alicia Landry—the only wife Tom Landry has ever had ▶

Rumor has it that some Cowboys fans would like to see their coach spend more effort on winning the Super Bowl and less on fighting obscenity and defending politicians.

But let's not push him. Without his outside interests, Tom Blandry just might develop an emotional approach to the game and become more like Chuck Noll, Bill Walsh, Tom Flores, Joe Gibbs, and other NFL coaches who really coach. And who have won Super Bowls since the Cowboys last made an appearance in the NFL classic.

★ GREAT PLAYS, MEMORABLE MOMENTS ★

The Cowboys put the writing on the wall for kicker Danny Villanueva, who led the Cowboys in scoring in 1965 and 1966. Villanueva also set the team record for most field goals in a game (4) in 1966 as well as most extra points for both a game and a season. So what have you done for us lately?, asked the Corporates.

In the spring of 1967, the Cowboys staged a "Kicking Karavan" in the U.S. and Europe, holding tryouts hoping to find someone to replace their record-setting kicker. Villanueva took on all comers and beat them all, but he didn't forget.

The following summer, Villanueva waited until the day before he was supposed to report to training camp to tell Landry—by telegram—that he was retiring. Tom, take this job and kick it!

"It was a team effort."

Win, lose, or draw, Dallas Coach Tom Landry has used that phrase, or a reasonable facsimile thereof, to describe his Cowboys' effort. The Dallas system is built around The Team. Nothing is as important as The Team.

All for one, one for all? Guess again.

Following the season-ending loss to the Los Angeles Rams in the 1983 NFC wildcard game, team spirit may have hit an all-time low in modern Cowboys history.

Who killed the Cowboys Team Spirit? We have more suspects than a Perry Mason mystery.

Your honor, for our first witness, we call to the stand backup quarterback Gary Hogeboom: "We have leadership problems. Coach Landry is a quiet-type coach and Danny (White) is a quiet-type person. I can see where we've had problems, though they don't stem from a certain individual."

Strong safety Dextor Clinkscale, who was benched for this playoff debacle in favor of rookie Bill Bates: "We gave up two touchdowns and a field goal on miscues by him (Bates). It's a team effort. But Bill was out there and inexperienced in his first playoff game. He made some mistakes and they cost us."

Butch Johnson, the classic "could-start-for-

TEAM SPIRIT

any-other-team-in-the-league" wide receiver: "There is a lack of team unity. He [Landry] has built up animosity between players on this team. He has pitted players against each other."

Landry traced the causes for the loss all the way back to the Dallas—Washington game three weeks earlier. Too much Cowboys emotion was squandered on that 31—10 shellacking.

Hogwash, said backup quarterback Hogeboom. "No way I buy that," he added. "I know everybody was working as hard as they could and I know things like this happen, but we weren't playing good football."

L.A. tight end Mike Barber echoed the sentiment: "They [the Cowboys] just didn't have that hustle, that sting or incentive it takes to win in the playoffs. I just couldn't see it in their faces. They didn't have that intensity."

In 1983, the Cowboys allegedly had it all. Size. Strength. Speed. Smarts. Talent. A quick computer. They had everything a team could want on paper.

But they had no spirit.

And who's to blame? Former President Harry Truman had a sign on his desk that read: "The Buck Stops Here."

Take a hint, Tom.

No! No! No! 1983 was not a vintage year for Cowboys team spirit. ▲

Rolaids Roger Staubach

No book about the Dallas Cowboys would be complete without a detailed section on Roger Staubach, ol' number 12, The Greatest Living Cowboy. So here are some twelve memorable moments in the life of Number 12.

1. When little Roger was in high school in Cincinnati, he wanted to play college ball for Notre Dame. But the Fighting Irish weren't interested in Roger even though he attended a Catholic boys school. Staubach shopped around for another school, and signed a national letter of intent with Purdue. Then Notre Dame came after Roger after his performance in the state high school all-star game, but Staubach turned them down. His word is his bond, right? Purdue had him fair and square, right?

Wrong. Roger decided to attend the Naval Academy.

2. Staubach had a history of problems with the English language long before he started misspelling "relief" in television commercials. Roger failed to meet the Naval Academy's entrance requirements in English and was sent to New Mexico Military Institute for a year to work on his grades. In his autobiography (for which he used a ghost writer, naturally), The Greatest Living Cowboy misspelled Fran Tarkenton's last name twice in the space of three lines. He must have confused Fran with author Booth Tarkington.

3. Nineteen sixty-three could well have been the best year The Greatest Living Cowboy ever had. He

No relief in sight; Coy brought home the Bacon for Washington and left Rolaids Roger a fallen star. ▶

quarterbacked Navy to a 9–1 record, a Number Two ranking, and a shot at the national championship against top-ranked Texas in the Cotton Bowl. He was drafted in the tenth round by the Cowboys as a future. And he won the Heisman Trophy as the best college football player in the country. Clint Murchison and Tom Landry got a good look at their future quarterback in the Cotton Bowl game on New Year's Day, 1964. With the national title hanging in the balance, Staubach and the Middies were stampeded by the Longhorns, 28–6. Ol' Roger wasn't exactly setting the Cotton Bowl on fire. Navy finished the year 9–2, with both losses coming in Dallas at the Cowboys' home stadium (the other Navy loss was against SMU in a game played in the Cotton Bowl). And what did Roger do for an encore after his Heisman Trophy year? He led Navy to a losing season.

4. The American Football League Kansas City Chiefs offered Roger a contract while he was still at the Academy. Roger made sure the Cowboys knew of the offer and a bidding war ensued. Murchison's counteroffer topped Lamar Hunt and the Chiefs,

Nobody does it better—Staubach left the ball on the ground more than any other Super Bowl player. ▶

45

and Roger took the Cowboys' money. He got a $10,000 signing bonus and $500 a month while serving on active duty in the Navy. Anchors aweigh!

5. Roger's Navy career was limited to being a supply officer in Vietnam. The Navy discovered he was color blind and wouldn't let him serve on ships or near an airplane. According to service regulations, he shouldn't have been admitted to the Academy in the first place. Bad English. Bad eyes. Good arm. His color blindness served him well in the NFL. Only 109 career interceptions.

6. Staubach said goodbye to the Navy on July 5, 1969. That's the same day Dandy Don announced his retirement. Roger's very first start as Cowboy quarterback was against the Colts the same year. Roger threw four interceptions. Baltimore won, 23–7. But the Greatest Living Cowboy would become a Super Bowl record setter. He holds Super Bowl records for career fumbles (five), most fumbles in a game (three), and most times sacked in a Super Bowl (seven).

7. Nineteen seventy-six was not Roger's best year. It began in training camp when former backup quarterback Clint Longley earned a spot in the heart of every Dallas hater when he sucker-punched The Greatest Living Cowboy in the locker room. Longley, who had fought once before with Staubach, caught him with a solid punch as Roger was taking his shoulder pads off. Staubach was momentarily knocked unconscious. Longley was soon traded.

Texas Monthly named Roger "Best Wimp."

8. In 1978, former CBS football analyst Alex Hawkins got in trouble for saying what many Cowboys haters already knew. Hawkins said that The Greatest Living Cowboy "kinda runs like a sissy."

9. When Roger won a free vacation for being named the most popular Cowboy by the fans, he told the contest sponsor he was too busy to take their trip and suggested they give it instead to some needy family. After Roger won the MVP award in the 1971 Super Bowl, he declined to accept a magazine's award of a new sports car. Give it to a needy family? Not quite. Roger wanted to trade it in for a station wagon.

10. Roger was known as a fierce competitor who hated to lose. Teammates didn't like to play games with Roger. Cornell Green didn't like playing basketball with him, because every time Cornell won a game Staubach wanted to play another. And another. And another. Until Roger won. Danny White beat Roger at table tennis during training camp one year and Staubach threw his paddle against the wall.

11. In 1980, Roger was an announcer for CBS and came down with a classic case of foot-in-mouth disease during a Dallas-St. Louis game. Real broadcaster Frank Gleiber asked Roger what the Cowboys had to do to stop the Cardinals offense. "In fact, I talked to my daughter Amy this morning

It's hard to run like a sissy when the other team won't let go. ◀

about it," began Roger, "and she said the Number One problem was the bomb." Roger's remark, closely resembling a comment made by President Jimmy Carter in a debate with Republican challenger Ronald Reagan, came just two days before election day. Roger had made campaign appearances for Reagan and other Republicans and his biased remarks infuriated Democrats. He later tried to extricate his foot by saying people just don't understand his sense of humor. Or his politics.

12. In his last NFL game, The Greatest Living Cowboy ended his career on this glorious note: His last pass was completed to a member of his own team, offensive guard Herbert Scott. An ineligible receiver. He went out like he came in: on a losing note. Dallas 19, Los Angeles 21.

Sex on the Sidelines

"Tell me, these women, are they wayward?"
—*Viktor Tikhonov, coach of the Russian national hockey team after seeing the Dallas Cowboys Cheerleaders*

Only a Russian would have to ask.

In 1972, when most NFL teams were still letting pimply high school girls in heavy sweaters and pleated skirts stand on the sidelines and wave only pompons, the Dallas Cowboys had a better idea: soften the violence on the field with a little sex on the sidelines.

So it came to pass that the Cowboys' brass selected seven nubile, leggy lasses, dressed them in cowgirl costumes so scanty they wouldn't cover a toy poodle, and told them to prance along the sidelines of the first Cowboys home game that season.

Television, not to mention the male fans, loved it. CBS cameramen became acrobats with their zoom lenses and the ritual of running to the kitchen for a cold brew during time outs was lost forever. Even the most ardent Dallas Cowboys hater could be forgiven for tuning in occasionally to watch those Texas dolls bump and grind with more moves than Allied Van Lines.

The Dallas Cowboys Cheerleaders became an overnight sensation and a blockbuster attraction for the Corporates. The Dallas Cowboys Cheerleaders did it all—calendars, posters, playing cards, television shows, personal appearances—and the seduction of John Q. Public was assured. The sultry beauties in sprayed-on shorts, cowboy boots, hats, and the most sensual halter tops seen this side of *Charlie's Angels* became the rage and scourge of the NFL.

"Of course they're sexy," understated Suzanne Mitchell, the Cheerleaders' director, choreographer, Mother Superior, and protector. "But what's wrong with that? Who wants to go to a game and look at ugly women?"

Suzanne, of course, is right, and the rest of the league soon fell in line with the Cowboys. The Honey Bears in Chicago, the Pony Express in Denver, the Embraceable Ewes in Los Angeles, and others soon held tryouts for the right to heat up the crowd and the television audience. The men, like the Russian hockey coach, wanted them to be "wayward" while the women had fantasies of themselves kicking and dancing in front of 60,000 cheering fans.

Although the Cowboys Cheerleaders attracted even more fans to the Silver-and-Blue Sissies, they also spawned a new group of bonafide Cowboys haters— the women of America.

Feminists were outraged at the raw display of sex and mocked the Cheerleaders as empty-headed dim-wits who let themselves become sex symbols.

If the uniforms weren't suggestive enough, the Corporates' front office did a real number on the type of girls who would fill out their skimpy outfits. They were all wholesome, fresh-faced, girl-next-door types. They were secretaries, college students, teachers, all "honored" to prance around the sidelines for $15 a game.

But the tough image of the Cowboys Cheerleaders was tarnished a time or two, even though the organiza-

The eyes of Texas E. Schramm are always on his leggy lovelies. ▲

tion took great pains to insure that the girls stayed out of trouble and out of controversy.

The Cheerleaders were forbidden to date or mingle with the football players. Ms. Mitchell made them practice extensively, sent them all to Dale Carnegie courses, and imposed a strict code of conduct on

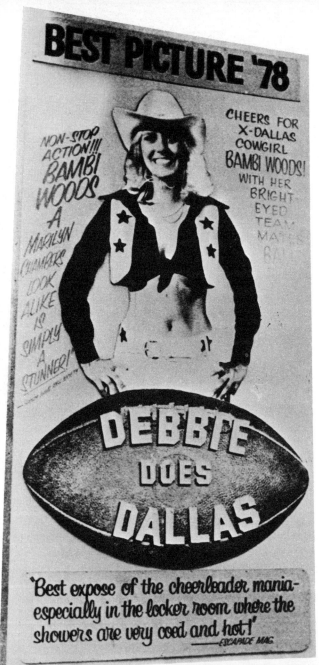

them. They can't be interviewed in their apartments. They must be high school graduates. There is to be no hanky-panky with the fans. Nothing to tarnish the image of the squeaky clean Cowboys, you know.

Everything was going smoothly until a little X-rated movie called *Debbie Does Dallas* was released.

Debbie *was* wayward.

Ol' Debbie did New York and Los Angeles and a lot of points in between, but she ran into trouble when she tried to do Big D. The 90-minute film about a woman hoping to try out for the Dallas Cowboys Cheerleaders and finding all sorts of erotic adventures was shown twice in Dallas in February 1979.

The Cowboys called the vice squad.

The Dallas Corporates filed suit claiming that *Debbie Does Dallas* was obscene and specifically objected to the similarity between the uniforms worn by Debbie and her mates and the real Dallas Cowboys Cheerleaders uniforms.

Ms. Mitchell testified at one hearing that the uniforms were identical except for the hat. (Who would ever notice the hat?)

A sympathetic judge, no doubt a Cowboys fan, ordered the makers of *Debbie Does Dallas* to edit out all references to the Cheerleaders and remove all pictures of the uniforms. The Corporate Cowboys and their sacred image were protected from the evils of the X-rated.

While the Cowboys claimed a courtroom triumph,

Debbie could do New York and L.A., but not Big D.

◄

the promoters of *Debbie Does Dallas* received millions in free national publicity.

But that wasn't the only time the Dallas Corporates have resorted to courtroom tactics to protect their image. They also went after an enterprising *Playboy* photographer who produced a darling poster of five former Cowboys Cheerleaders wearing the familiar blue-and-white outfits *sans* the halter tops. Chalk up another win for the Corporates—and a loss for good taste—when a California judge ordered the posters destroyed.

Then there is the sad story of the Cowboys and a group of former Cheerleaders who banded together to form the Dallas Cowgirls.

Jeanie Cavett and Patty Taylor decided to form the group to work trade shows, model, and make public appearances. Some of them even posed for *Playboy*. The Cowboys reacted in typical good humor. They went to court to get an injunction preventing the Cowgirls from imitating the Cowboys Cheerleaders.

Ms. Cavett's reaction was succinct. The Cowboys organization, she said, is "trying to make us look like scum."

Suzanne Mitchell contended the Cowgirls group "doesn't stand for what we stand for." She said the Cowgirls are "deceiving the fans who look at us for a certain image and for certain values."

Ms. Mitchell also had these comments about her two former charges and their new group: "You know what

Mommie dearest: In the words of Suzanne, "Who wants to look at ugly women?" ▶

our organization is like," she said. "We like to do things one way around here. It's like a mother-child relationship. I was awfully close to them at one time and it hurts to see them turning this around and degrading the things we taught them in the first place."

The "mother-child" relationship was strained indeed. Ms. Cavett's Cowboys "mother" didn't see fit to call and discuss the situation. Ms. Cavett read she was being sued in the newspaper.

The case was settled when the Dallas Cowgirls agreed to change their name to the Dallas Girls, take the blue stars off their tight-fitting pants, and provide a disclaimer on all advertising and promotional material.

The Cowboys wanted much more. "They wanted the girls to change the color of the uniforms and we told them to stuff it," said Ms. Cavett's lawyer, Mark Jordan Siegel. "They're arrogant and try to big-boy you to death. Those women are entitled to make a living. There's nothing wrong with a little competition in this country. If you're driving a Buick down the street and somebody thinks it's an Oldsmobile, it's not Buick's fault."

Ms. Cavett and Ms. Taylor believe what the Cowboys are really doing is trying to prevent them from making a living.

"It's just like an ex-football player using his name to start his own business," Ms. Cavett said. "No one can take away the fact that we were once cheerleaders for the Cowboys. And because of that, people want to meet us. We're not doing anything wrong. Suzanne knew we were in business for about two years and she didn't say a thing. But when she turned down a TV commercial, the company called us and we did the commercial. That was it. The next thing I know it's in the newspaper that the Cowboys were mad and I got served legal papers the same day. They never said anything to me. But they would call clients and try to scare them off. It certainly doesn't help business."

There also was the time the Cowboys were embarrassed by a man who dressed up as a cheerleader and showed up on the sidelines of Texas Stadium.

Barry Bremen, a strapping six-foot-four insurance salesman from Michigan, strolled the sidelines dressed like a Cowboys Cheerleader (YUK!). He might have gotten away with it if he hadn't tried to dance with the real Cheerleaders in the closing minutes of a Dallas-Washington game.

Once again, the Cowboys' legal beagles sprang into action. The team filed a suit against Bremen and asked the court to ban him from Texas Stadium for life (they call that punishment?), and sought $5,000 in damages from him for trespassing and creating a nuisance.

In 1982, the Cowboys and their Cheerleaders were at it again. This time they got involved in politics.

The National Conservative Political Action Committee, or NCPAC, filmed a political ad at Texas Stadium showing models dressed like the hallowed Cheerleaders. The women showed little enthusiasm for incumbent U.S. Senator Lloyd Bentsen, a Texas Democrat, while an announcer recalled the Senator's voting record.

NCPAC, which was backing Bentsen's Republican challenger, U.S. Rep. Jim Collins of Dallas, aired the commercials in West Texas and the Cowboys kicked off another court case.

Although several members of the Cowboys, including coach Tom Landry, had endorsed Collins, the team demanded that the political ad be taken off the air because it infringed on the Cheerleaders trademark and reputation. The Corporates won again.

Sex, courtroom drama, and more sex. All the ingredients for boob-tube success.

But truth did triumph when a former Dallas Cowboys Cheerleader set the record straight.

"We were selling sex," she said. "They would pull our shorts up higher on our legs so our butts would show.

We were required to wear push-up bras. The whole thing revolved around butts and cleavage. For them to say we were good little virgin girls is ludicrous.

"During one game, one of the girls was doing a cheer and one of her breasts popped right out of her uniform. The crowd loved it. That's what we were there for."

Luckily for the Cheerleader flasher, the Cowboys didn't sue her. Not yet, anyway.

But that wouldn't be in the "best interest of the game." Only the Cowboys could turn something as great as sex into yet another item on the team's computer checklist.

"Tell me. These women. Are they wayward?"

Every girl's dream—fifteen dollars a game and a sideline seat to boot▼

All-Time Cowboys Killer Team

America is full of people who talk down the Cowboys, but you've got to put your heart and soul into Cowboy-hating to make the All-Time Cowboys Killer Team. These gentlemen more than qualify.

Coach: *George Allen, Washington Redskins.* When he was coaching the Washington Redskins from 1971 to 1977, Allen turned hating the Dallas Cowboys into a religious experience. He made it personal. The Cowboys, with their computerized organization, didn't know how to react. They accused him of spying, lying and cheating. Allen's Redskins beat Dallas the first time they played and they whipped the Cowboys on six other occasions, including the 26–3 humiliation of the Cowboys in the 1972 NFC championship. To add insult to injury, Allen compiled a personal list of pro football's 25 Greatest Games and listed six games involving Dallas among his greatest. Naturally, all six were Dallas losses.

Offense
Quarterback: *Bart Starr, Green Bay Packers.* Starr earns a place on the team for having led his Packers to consecutive NFL titles over the Cowboys in 1966 and 1967. His most memorable moment, and one of the all-time great plays for Dallas haters, came in the 1967 game in Green Bay when Starr scored the winning touchdown on a quarterback sneak with only 13 seconds left in the game. Starr is the offensive captain of the All-Time Cowboys Killer team.

Running Back: *Wilbert Montgomery, Philadelphia Eagles.* This Philadelphia Eagle played college football for Abilene Christian in Texas and helped his teammates knock the Cowboys out of yet another Super Bowl appearance. Montgomery left his mark on "America's Team" in the 1980 NFC title game by rushing for 194 yards. The Eagles humbled the Cowboys 20–7.

Running Back: *Franco Harris, Pittsburgh Steelers.* In two Super Bowl victories over the Cowboys, Harris rushed for 150 yards, caught two passes for 48 yards, and scored a touchdown.

Wilbert Montgomery: "America's Team" was no match for this Philadelphia Eagle. ▼

George Allen: He made it personal.▶

Wide Receiver: *Dwight Clark, San Francisco 49ers.* The San Francisco receiver endeared himself to Cowboys haters in the 1982 NFC title game. With only 51 seconds left to play, Clark stretched for a fingertip catch in the back of the end zone to seal a 28–27 49er victory. Clark and quarterback Joe Montana combined for two TDs as San Francisco knocked the Cryboys out of the race for the Super Bowl.

Dwight Clark: His last-minute stretch left the Cowboys hopping mad. (Photo by Phil Huber) ▼

Wide Receiver: *Lynn Swann, Pittsburgh Steelers.* Dallas tried everything to stop Swann in two Super Bowls with little success. Cliff Harris threatened to take his head off and Benny Barnes tried tripping him, but the graceful Steeler couldn't be intimidated or stopped. He caught a 64-yard TD pass in Super Bowl X as Pittsburgh claimed a 21–17 victory. In Super Bowl XIII, Swann was even more brilliant, grabbing seven passes for 124 yards and a touchdown. The Steelers won, 35–31.

Wide Receiver *(Honorable mention): Harold Jackson, Los Angeles Rams.* October 14, 1973 will long live in the memory of Dallas Cowboys haters. Little Harold caught seven passes for 238 yards and four touchdowns. He showed Tom Landry that one individual *can* make a difference in a team sport as the Rams won, 37–31.

Tight End: *Jackie Smith, Dallas Cowboys and St. Louis Cardinals.* O.K., so he played for the Cowboys. But the former St. Louis Cardinal once helped his club humiliate the Cowboys 38–0. Cowboys haters best remember Smith for dropping a sure touchdown pass from Roger Staubach in Super Bowl XIII. The Cowboys settled for a field goal and lost the Super Bowl trophy to Pittsburgh by four points.

Tight End *(Honorable mention): John Mackey, Baltimore Colts.* For all you perfectionists who object to the selection of Smith. Mackey never played for the Cowboys and was a true Cowboys Killer in Super Bowl V. Baltimore's legendary Johnny Unitas threw a pass at wide receiver Eddie Hinton, but Dallas's Mel Renfro tipped the ball. An alert Mackey plucked the ball out of the air and sprinted untouched into the end zone. The 75-yard play earned Mackey a special place in the hearts of Cowboys haters everywhere. Baltimore won the game, 16–13.

Center: *Ken Bowman, Green Bay Packers.* Bowman was the unsung hero of Green Bay's 1967 Ice Bowl victory. The burly center helped Jerry Kramer execute a double-team block on Cowboy defensive tackle Jethro Pugh. Bart Starr followed the blocks into the end zone for the historic touchdown.

Guard: *Jerry Kramer, Green Bay Packers.* Kramer and center Ken Bowman knocked Jethro Pugh on his frozen keister, allowing Bart Starr to sneak across the goal line for the decisive TD in the 1967 NFL title game. Thanks to television's instant replay, Kramer became an overnight celebrity and even wrote a book about the championship season entitled, what else, *Instant Replay*. Jethro Pugh did not write a book.

Guard: *Conrad Dobler, St. Louis Cardinals.* No easy way to say it: Dobler was a dirty football player. Players knew it. Coaches knew it. Fans knew it. Dobler enjoyed the reputation. His election to the Cowboys Killers was unanimous. In a game against Dallas, safety Cliff Harris was sitting on the ground. Dobler got a 10-yard head of steam and lowered the proverbial boom on the dismounted Cowboy. Harris was taken off the field on a stretcher and Dobler's reputation grew. While this does not technically qualify Dobler as a Cowboys Killer, it

(Left) *Jackie Smith: No hands. No feet. No Super Bowl ring.*

(Right) *Jerry Kramer: Jethro Pugh can close his eyes today and still see* Instant Replay. ▲

certainly puts him at the top of the list of Cowboys Disablers.

Tackle: *George Starke, Washington Redskins.* The Cowboys signed Starke as a free agent out of Columbia University, but didn't think enough of him to keep him on the roster. The Redskins picked him up and Starke has become a mainstay in the vaunted "Hogs" offensive line. In 1982 and 1983, Starke helped keep the names of Cowboys off the Super Bowl roster.

Tackle: *Dick Schafrath, Cleveland Browns.* This stalwart of the Browns' offensive line had a field day in 1963, helping a running back by the name of Jim Brown run over, around and through the Cowboys. Brown rolled up 232 yards and scored on romps of 71 and 62 yards as the Browns humbled Dallas 41–24. Schafrath was a six-time All-Pro selection and the Browns had a 14–6 record against Dallas during his days in the offensive trenches. The 232-yard day enjoyed by Brown still stands as the single-game rushing record against the Dallas defense.

Kicker: *Jim O'Brien, Baltimore Colts.* The Cryboys watched helplessly as O'Brien won Super Bowl V for the Baltimore Colts by booting a 32-yard field goal with just five seconds left in the game. It was the first of three Super Bowl losses for Dallas.

Defense

End: *Dexter Manley, Washington Redskins.* In 1983, this Texas native was instrumental in helping the Cowboys lose their third straight NFC title game. Just before the end of the first half, the Washington end executed a favorite Cowboys Killer tackle, one putting Cryboy quarterback Danny White out of the game with a concussion. In the second half, Mr. D intimidated backup quarterback Gary Hogeboom, tipping a screen pass that teammate Darryl Grant turned into a touchdown. Washington whomped Dallas 31–27.

End: *Billy Ray Smith, Baltimore Colts.* This stalwart defensive end from the Colts was the man who made Cowboy running back Duane Thomas fumble on the Baltimore two-yard line in Super Bowl V. Dallas was ahead at the time, 13–6. Colts linebacker Mike Curtis recovered the ball, thanks to Smith yelling at the referees, "Colts' ball! Colts' ball!" Naturally, the Cowboys are still crying about the call by the official. But the fumble helped the Colts tie the game and set up Jim O'Brien's field goal.

End *(honorable mention): Willie Davis, Green Bay Packers.* Davis was the mainstay of a demonic defense that helped the Green Bay Packers to two NFL title victories over Dallas. But his Cowboys Killer status was assured during a 1968 regular-season game that Green Bay won 28–17. Davis yanked Don Meredith's helmet down with such force that it broke Dandy's nose. Meredith left the game briefly and was booed heartily by know-nothing Dallas fans when he returned.

Tackle: *Darryl Grant, Washington Redskins.* The big Redskin tackle picked off a tipped screen pass from Gary Hogeboom in the 1983 NFC title game and rumbled into the end zone to clinch the Washington win.

Tackle: *Diron Talbert, Washington Redskins.* Talbert was a member of George Allen's Over-The-Hill-Gang. He developed and nurtured a deep dislike of Roger Staubach. In 1975, stories surfaced about homosexuality in pro football. Talbert called Staubach a "fag" during a game. By Staubach's own admission,

Darryl Grant: If Tony Dorsett can't hold the football, what makes you think he can hold a defensive tackle? ▲

Talbert "brought out the worst" in Roger. In fact, Talbert was the only man in the NFL to ever make Staubach cuss on the football field. For making even saintly Roger give up the moral high ground and get down in the trenches with the *real* football players, Talbert is the defensive captain of the All-Time Cowboys Killer Team.

★ GREAT PLAYS, MEMORABLE MOMENTS ★

Fumbling is a time-honored Dallas tradition. In 1964, Don Meredith set an NFL record for the most fumbles in a season (16). In 1981, Danny White tied an NFL record for the most own fumbles recovered in a season (8). Not to be outdone, Tony Dorsett holds (until he fumbles it) the NFL record for most career playoff fumbles (13).

Captain Diron Talbert: It took a real Texan to make Roger cuss. ▼

Tackle *(honorable mention): Mel Tom, Philadelphia Eagles.* In a 1971 game against the Philadelphia Eagles, Roger Staubach dropped back to throw his first pass of the game. Roger should have dodged. Tom unloaded a lethal forearm to Staubach's head, knocking Roger out of the game and a few years closer to Rolaids commercials. Staubach was so upset that he

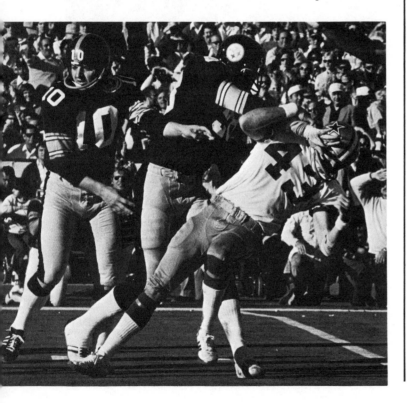

told a Dallas sportswriter that he planned to use his four years of Navy hand-to-hand combat training and get even with Tom. After the story was printed, a more sensible Staubach claimed he had been "joking." Ha, ha.

Linebacker: *Marlin McKeever, Los Angeles Rams.* In a 1971 preseason game, McKeever caught Roger Staubach scrambling out of the pocket and made him pay. Captain Sissy suffered a severe shoulder separation that kept him on the sidelines for most of the season.

Linebacker: *Jack Lambert, Pittsburgh Steelers.* Lambert's Steelers whipped the Cowboys in two Super Bowls, but the one play that put him on the Killer Team occurred in Super Bowl X. Steelers kicker Roy Gerela had just missed a field goal and Cowboy safety Cliff Harris patted Gerela on the helmet and muttered a few sweet nothings in his ear. Lambert ran up to Harris, lifted him off the ground, and threw him to the turf. In front of God, Tom Landry and a Super Bowl audience.

Linebacker: *Dave Robinson, Green Bay Packers.* In the closing moments of the 1966 title game, Dallas was knocking on the Green Bay goal line. On fourth-and-goal from the two, Don Meredith rolled out to pass, and Robinson rolled out to meet him, forcing a desperation pass that Green Bay intercepted to preserve a dreamy

Jack Lambert: Touch my kicker and I'll rearrange your face. ◀

34–27 victory. For the Cowboys, the bad dream continued. Robinson continued to harass the Crybabys as a member of George Allen's Redskins.

Defensive Back: *Ken Houston, Washington Redskins.* Cowboys haters worth their venom will never forget the tackle Houston laid on Dallas running back Walt Garrison. Houston met Garrison inches from the goal line and stopped him cold to help Washington skin the Cowboys 14–7 in 1973 at RFK Stadium. Two years later, Houston picked off a Roger Staubach pass to stop a Dallas drive during a 30–24 Redskins overtime win.

Defensive Back: *Tom Brown, Green Bay Packers.* When Dave Robinson forced Don Meredith to fling that fatal pass in the 1966 title game, Brown hauled in the wobbly effort for an interception that iced the Green Bay victory.

Defensive Back: *Bobby Bryant, Minnesota Vikings.* When the Vikes pillaged the Cowboys in the 1973 NFC title game, Bryant picked off a Staubach pass and returned it 63 yards for a score. Minnesota 27, Dallas 10.

Defensive Back: *LeRoy Irvin, Los Angeles Rams.* LeRoy will be dreaming of a White Christmas for years after intercepting one of the Danny White's passes and romping an NFC playoff record 94 yards. He didn't score on the play, but he would have if a gimpy leg hadn't slowed him down. Don't you love it? A defensive back with an injured leg intercepted a pass and ran 94 yards before the stunned Cowboys could recover. Final score in that 1983 classic: Los Angeles 24, Dallas 17.

Defensive Back *(honorable mention): Al Nelson, Philadelphia Eagles.* Al caught the Cowboys sleeping and made them pay to the tune of an NFL-record missed field goal return. Nelson hauled in the errant attempt and set sail. He stopped 101 yards later, with a TD and a record to his credit.

Special Awards

Fred Swearingen, NFL Zebra. Fantastic Fred was the eagle-eyed official who flagged Benny Barnes for tripping Steeler receiver Lynn Swann in Super Bowl XIII. All

Fred Swearingen (back to camera): He's one zebra with sharp eyes, deaf ears. ▼

GREATEST COWBOYS KILLER TEAMS

Of course, won—lost records point to the greatest Cowboys Killer Teams. Below are the clubs that historically have the Cowboys' number.

Overall		*Postseason Only*	
Cleveland	*15—8*	*Baltimore*	*2—0**
Pittsburgh	*12—10*	*Pittsburgh*	*2—0*
LA Rams	*10—9**	*Washington*	*2—0*
Green Bay	*8—4*	*Philadelphia*	*1—0*
LA/Oakland Raiders	*2—1*	*Cleveland*	*2—1*
		Green Bay	*2—1*

*Includes games that the Cowboys media guide does not include in overall records against Dallas. Both are NFL Playoff Bowls. The Cowboys were in two and lost both; a 1966 thriller to Baltimore, 35—3; and a 1969 appearance against the LA Rams, which ended in a 31—0 embarrassment.

the Cowboys thought the penalty was going to be against Swann, but Fred fooled 'em. Swearingen had the guts to call it right.

Sy Ullsperger, Green Bay. He didn't wear a helmet, run with the ball, throw or catch a pass, but was nevertheless instrumental in helping the Packers win the 1967 NFL title game over the Cowboys. Who is Sy Ulls-perger? He was the National Weather Service forecaster who predicted a cold air mass from Canada would bring sub-Arctic conditions to Green Bay by game time. He was right and the Packers were ready. It was minus-13 degrees at kickoff with a wind chill of minus-40 degrees. Dallas choked on a big, cold one, 21—17.

9

All-Time Worst Cowboys

Would-be football players are plentiful around Dallas, and trying to compile an all-time worst team is like trying to *not* find a star at the Academy Awards show. So, may we have the envelopes please . . .

Offense

Quarterback: *Sonny Gibbs,* taken in the second round of the 1962 draft, was the first college player selected by Dallas that year. At 6′7″ from Texas Christian University in neighboring Fort Worth, Gibbs figured high in the Cowboys' plans. But Gibbs lasted only one season with the Cowboys. In 1963, he played only one down in preseason and none in the regular season.

Running Back: *Claxton Welch* was second-team All-

PAC Eight behind O. J. Simpson before he signed with the Cowboys in 1968 out of the University of Oregon. The highlight of his three-year stint with Dallas came in 1971 when he rushed 14 times for 51 yards and one touchdown for the season, giving him a total of 85 yards for his brief NFL career.

Running Back: *Bill Thomas* was the Cowboys' first-round draft choice out of Boston College in 1972. Coach Tom Landry compared him to Calvin Hill and Duane Thomas. The rest of the NFL compared him to Calvin Coolidge and Marlo Thomas. Thomas played only one season in Dallas. He still carries the distinction of being one of Gil Brandt's all-time worst first-round draft choices.

Sonny Gibbs: The bigger they are, the harder they fall. He came in the second round, and left after one season. ▲

Wide Receiver: *Ola Lee Murchison* was the first college track star to play for the Cowboys. He was signed as a free agent in 1961 out of the University of the Pacific after Dallas scouts were impressed with his 9.7 speed in the 100-yard dash. His career was about as fast. He lasted only one year with the Cowboys.

Wide Receiver: *Dennis Homan* played in the shadow of All-America Ray Perkins at the University of Alabama. But the Cowboys thought of him as a diamond in the rough and made him their first-round draft choice in 1968. As a rookie, Homan caught a measly four passes and scored one TD. His second season wasn't much better, with 12 catches. By 1971, the diamond was back in the rough. Another first-round draft choice down the tubes.

Tight End: *Lee Folkins* came to the Cowboys from Green Bay after the 1962 College All-Star Game in which he took a swing at a college player, missed, and knocked out the head linesman. After three years of his dropping passes, Dallas traded him to the Steelers where he came back to haunt the Cowboys. During a Pittsburgh-Dallas game, a Cowboy dropped the kickoff and Folkins was there to pick it up. He ran the ball into the end zone for the touchdown and kept going toward the Dallas bench. When he got to Tom Landry, Folkins tossed the ball to his old coach and kept on going.

Center: *Robert Shaw* was a 6'4", 254-pound center at Tennessee when the Cowboys made him their first-round draft choice in 1979. The coaching staff thought that Shaw, the first center ever drafted number one by

Dallas, would be the successor to veteran John Fitzgerald. But Shaw suffered a rash of injuries including a knee injury in the second game of the 1981 season that ended his career.

(Left) *Ola Lee Murchison: No kin to Clint*

(Center) *Joe Bob Isbell: He brought the plays in from the sidelines and sometimes remembered them.*

(Right) *Andy Cvercko: It's not every lineman who's worth eight points on one play.* ▼

Guard: *Joe Bob Isbell* was the Cowboys' first messenger guard. In a 1962 game against the Lions, Don Meredith changed the play that Isbell brought in from Landry to a trap play. Isbell got confused, as did guard Andy Cvercko. As a result, both guards pulled in opposite directions and had a head-on collision.

Guard: *Andy Cvercko* helped the Cowboys to become the first team in memory in the NFL to actually *lose* points on a touchdown. In a 1962 game against the Steelers, Dallas quarterback Eddie LeBaron retreated to his own end zone and threw a bomb to Frank

Clarke for what should have been a 99-yard TD. But Cvercko was caught holding in the end zone and under an obscure rule the touchdown was wiped out and Pittsburgh was awarded a safety. Dallas lost the game by those two points.

Tackle: *Jim Boeke* was the Cowboys' starting left tackle in the 1966 NFL championship game against Green Bay. With the Packers clinging to a seven-point lead and only 1:52 left in the game, Dallas had a second-and-goal on the Packers' one-yard line when Boeke was caught jumping offsides. Now operating from the six-yard line, Meredith threw an incomplete pass on the next play. After completing a five-yarder to Pettis Norman on third down, Dandy was intercepted on fourth down as Dallas lost. Boeke, who once was Ricky Nelson's bodyguard when the teen idol toured Japan, also was in the movie *North Dallas Forty*. He played the lineman named Stallings who was berated by the Landry-like coach during a review of game films and then cut. Typecasting.

Tackle: *Bruce Walton* was the Cowboys' fifth-round draft choice out of UCLA in 1973. At 6'7" and 251 pounds, he should have been a ferocious defender. He wasn't. He lasted three years with the Cowboys and then went back to California where he once had a minor role in a Walt Disney movie. Oh yes, his brother, Bill Walton, turned out to be quite a basketball player for UCLA.

Kicker: *Allen Green*, who was with the Cowboys in 1961, is remembered for what may be the all-time worst field goal attempt in the history of the NFL. In a 1961 game, Green lined up for a 20-yard field goal attempt that would have given Dallas one of their rare victories. Somehow, he managed to shank the kick and it wound up hitting not the crossbar or the upright, but the flag at the corner of the goal line.

Kick Returner: *Amos Marsh* and all-time Cowboy rusher Tony Dorsett have one thing in common: they have trouble hanging onto the football. In one game, Amos stood waiting to catch a high spiralling punt. He drew a bead on it, thought it was his and suddenly it hit him, smacking the top of his helmet.

★ GREAT PLAYS, MEMORABLE MOMENTS ★

The pressure of playoff competition can be fierce. This is the time the cream rises. Well, Cowboy kicker Mike Clark carefully placed the wet, muddy football on the tee in the 1969 Eastern Conference title game against Cleveland. The Cowboys were behind late in the game, and Landry ordered an onside kick. Clark stepped back, signalled the referee he was ready, and approached the ball. He slipped, whiffed the ball, and fell in the mud.

Teammates immediately nicknamed Clark "Onside."

Defense
Defensive End: *Tody Smith* was the first defensive lineman drafted by the Cowboys in the first round since

Bob Lilly. But Tody was no Lilly. He wasn't even as good as his awesome brother, Bubba Smith. Other NFL teams bypassed him because he suffered an injury his senior year at USC and played only four games. Dallas took a chance and he turned out to be one of their biggest first-round flops. Smith played three years in Dallas before he was shipped to Houston after a contract dispute.

Defensive End: *Larry Bethea* proved once again that Gil Brandt isn't the scout of defensive talent he's cracked up to be. Although Bethea was the Big Ten MVP at Michigan State and the Cowboys' number-one pick in the 1978 draft, he's spent more time on the bench than on the field. When Ed "Too Tall" Jones left the Cowboys to pursue a boxing career in 1979, the Cowboys coaches thought Bethea could take up the slack. He couldn't cut it. He was sent back to his familiar spot on the bench and the Cowboys traded for John Dutton. Bethea heeded the call back to Michigan, signing with the USFL Michigan Panthers in 1983.

Defensive Tackle: *Jethro Pugh* was an 11th-round draft choice from Elizabeth City State in 1965. So what if he went on to be on the Cowboys' defensive stalwarts? When they really needed him, he failed. Guess who Green Bay blocked in the 1967 NFL championship game that let Bart Starr sneak into the end zone to ice the victory over Dallas? Attaboy, Jethro.

Defensive Tackle: *Willie Townes*, a second-round

Jethro Pugh: It's a cold, cold world out there. ▶

67

(Left) *Randy White: Landry's attempt to turn an all-pro defensive tackle into a mediocre linebacker left a sour taste in his mouth.*

(Right) *Benny Barnes: He can trip with the best of 'em.* ▲

draft choice from Tulsa in 1966, was best known for sitting at Tom Landry's "Fat Man's Table" during training camps. Bob Lilly wrote that Townes "pretty well ate his way out of the league."

Linebacker: *Randy White* was the Cowboys' first-round draft choice out of Maryland in 1975, where he was an All-America lineman. But Tom Landry envisioned him as another Sam Huff, whom young Tom converted to a future Hall of Fame middle linebacker

while a Giants assistant in the 1950s. Everyone in Dallas knew Landry needed to come up with a replacement for retiring Cowboy linebacker Lee Roy Jordan. But the man Charlie Waters called "Manster"—half-man, half-monster—never mastered the position. Then Dallas tried to make White an outside linebacker. But he couldn't cut that either. Landry gave up his great experiment and White returned to the defensive line, where he's a perennial All-Pro. Randy White is one first-round pick who survived Landry's coaching.

Linebacker: *Steve Kiner* came out of Tennessee as a third-round draft choice in 1970. His rough and tumble reputation preceded him when he was arrested at a Knoxville rock concert for allegedly hitting an off-duty cop over the head with a folding chair. The highlight of his Cowboys career was catching a 14-yard pass from Dan Reeves on a fake field goal in 1970, the only year he played for Dallas. He might have played longer, but he couldn't play defense with a folding chair.

Linebacker: *John Babinecz* was a second-round draft choice in 1972 from Villanova. He played two years for the Cowboys and once recovered a fumble.

Cornerback: *Benny "Tripper" Barnes* is still crying about a tripping penalty against him in Super Bowl XIII. Barnes found the only way to stop Lynn Swann from eating him alive was to get his feet tangled with the Steelers' star receiver. The result was 33-yard penalty that led to a Steeler TD.

Cornerback: *Rod Hill* quickly earned the nickname

"Shrine Game" from his teammates because of his tendency to return punts east and west. As a rookie in 1982, he had a key fumble in the title game against the Redskins. The first-rounder now returns kicks only in emergencies.

Safety: *Aaron Mitchell* was a second-round draft choice from Nevada-Las Vegas in 1979. Bad gamble by the Cowboys. He lasted only two years with Dallas, where he is best remembered for inventing the "wave-and-run" pass defense. He would wave at receivers as they ran by him. He flagged opposing receivers for two years before the Cowboys finally got rid of him.

Safety: *Wade Manning* didn't even play football at Ohio State. But super scout Gil Brandt heard Manning was a hitter. He was—with a bat. But the great-hitting centerfielder couldn't make the switch from the diamond to the gridiron and lasted only one year with Dallas. Cowboys fans have lots of memories of Manning, mostly of seeing him chasing opponents into the end zone.

Punter: *Colin Ridgway* was a transplanted Australian whose nickname was "Boomer." As in boomerang. In a 1966 preseason game, Dallas was at its own 15-yard line on fourth down. Ridgway boomed one that went straight up and then began curling back. A San Francisco 49ers lineman fielded the "kick" and ran the five-yard punt back four yards to the Dallas 16-yard line.

Honorary Captain: *Tommy Loy* has played a

trumpet solo of "The Star-Spangled Banner" at every Cowboys home game since 1967. Too bad Tommy wasn't in Green Bay in 1967 for the famous Ice Bowl. He'd still be trying to get his lips off that sour-toned horn of his.

Colin Ridgway: "Boomer" was a kicker who couldn't. ▼

THE ONES THAT GOT AWAY

A nanosecond, in computer technology, is one billionth of a second. That's fast. And that's about the time it takes the Cowboys' computer to decide the fate of a football player. The Cowboys pride themselves on their brilliant scouting operation, their know-everything computer that evaluates every player in minute detail and spits out the subsequent Dallas draft choices. Of course, the Cowboys also pride themselves on the undrafted free agents who make the squad, like Drew Pearson, Everson Walls and Cornell Green. This means the Cowboys must be making some God-awful draft picks or overlooking some awfully talented players.

Let's take a look at some of the players Dallas decided to trade or simply cut from the roster. These were the players just a nanosecond or so away from wearing the Silver-and-Blue.

Todd Christensen, tight end, Los Angeles Raiders: He was Dallas's second draft choice in 1978. The huge running back from Brigham Young was nicknamed "Toddzilla." The Cowboys tried to make him a tight end, then traded him to the New York Giants. He was picked up by the Raiders a year later, led the NFL in receptions in 1983, and was everybody's All-Pro as well as a Super Bowl champ.

Steve DeBerg, quarterback, Tampa Bay Buccaneers: In 1977, DeBerg and another rookie quarterback, Glenn Carano, were vying for the third-string job on the Cowboys depth chart. Landry decided to keep Carano and sent DeBerg to San Francisco, where he became a starter until Joe Montana came along. DeBerg was then traded to Denver where former Cowboys assistant coach Dan Reeves was running the show. Carano, by the way, signed with the USFL in 1983 after spending most of 1982 holding for extra points and field goals and watching Danny White throw interceptions.

George Starke, offensive tackle, Washington Redskins: Starke signed with the Cowboys as a free agent out of Columbia. He never made it out of training camp. The Washington Redskins picked him up and he's been a stalwart for them for the past ten years. A member of the All-Time Cowboys Killers Team.

Jim Zorn, quarterback, Seattle Seahawks: He was the last player cut by the Cowboys in 1976. Landry had to decide between Zorn and Clint Longley. Landry went with the rattlesnake hunter from Abilene. Zorn was picked up by the Seahawks and became their starting quarterback. He was named the AFC Offensive Rookie of the Year and the AFC Player of the Year.

Raul Allegre, kicker, Baltimore Colts: Allegre is regarded as one of the best young kickers in the NFL. He was cut by Dallas in 1983 and traded to the Colts for a ninth-round draft choice. Allegre won five games for the Colts with his talented leg. He gets excellent distance and could break the NFL record for the longest field goal. The Cowboys really booted this one.

Ron Jessie, wide receiver, Detroit Lions and Los Angeles Rams: He was Dallas's eighth-round draft choice in 1971 out of Kansas State. The Cowboys didn't keep him. He signed with the Lions and had a brilliant career from 1971 to 1974. He also haunted the Cowboys as a member of the Rams from 1975 to 1979.

E. J. Holub, center and linebacker, Dallas Texans and Kansas City Chiefs: He was the Cowboys' second draft choice in 1961. Bob Lilly was their first pick that year. Holub decided to sign with the Dallas Texans of the AFL and became a perennial All-Pro. Bad knees ended his linebacking days, but the former Texas Tech Red Raider moved to center and anchored the offensive line for the Texans-turned-Chiefs.

Mac Percival, kicker, Chicago Bears: Percival was a kicker for Texas Tech when Gil Brandt and Ermal Allen discovered him in 1967 during a "Kicking Karavan." (If they had such a great scouting system, why did they need a "Kicking Karavan?") Percival signed with the Cowboys, was traded to the Bears and became Chicago's third all-time leading scorer behind George Blanda and Walter Payton. Percival holds the Bears' records for lifetime field goals, field goals in a season and field goals in a game.

(Left) *Todd Christensen: "Todzilla" traded in his Cowboys' star for a Super Bowl ring.*

(Right) *E. J. Holub: This Texan became a big Chief.* ▲

The Dallas Cowboys Haters' Trivia Quiz

Now that you've read 71 pages, let's see if you've learned anything. Correct answers and a scoring system follow.

1. Which teams played the first professional football game in Dallas?
   a. Cowboys-Colts
   b. Cowboys-Steelers
   c. Texans-Chargers
   d. Texans-Giants
   e. Texas-Oklahoma

2. What year was the first pro game played in Dallas?
   a. 1960
   b. 1961
   c. 1952

   d. 1955
   e. Still waiting

3. The expansion Cowboys were the epitome of defeat. How long did it take them to win a regular-season game?
   a. Two seasons
   b. Two games
   c. Twelve games
   d. Eight games

4. Why will the Cowboys forever be indebted to the late George Halas of the Chicago Bears?
   a. He kept the NFL from putting a franchise in Fort Worth.
   b. He gave the Cowboys his three best players in

the expansion draft.

c. He drafted Don Meredith and traded him to Dallas.

d. He declined to become the Cowboys' first coach.

5. In addition to the hole in the roof, what other unique feature did Texas Stadium have that no other NFL stadium could claim?

a. A drive-in theater in the parking lot.

b. It's the site of the annual Billy Graham crusade.

c. They discovered oil under the 50-yard line.

d. They use dollar bills for toilet paper.

e. All of the above

Did you hear the one about the Aggie who paid $20 million for a house with a hole in the roof? ▼

6. Why did the Cowboys management recently reprimand some of their fans?

a. They showed too much emotion at a game.

b. They spat tobacco juice on the field.

c. Their dates were grazing on the artificial turf.

d. Their limousines took up too many parking spaces.

7. In a classic show of Texas gaudiness, how much did a private box at Texas Stadium recently sell for?

a. $1 million

b. $250,000

c. $600,000

d. Two oil wells, 500 polled Herefords and four season tickets

e. A hot tub weekend with the Cheerleaders

8. What was Cowboys Vice-President for Personnel Development Gil Brandt's profession before he joined the team?

a. Basketball coach

b. Baby photographer

c. Fuller Brush man

d. Used car salesman

9. What do Gil Brandt and former Cowboys owner Clint Murchison have in common besides their affiliation with the Cowboys?

a. They were campaign advisers to Richard Nixon

b. They have the same birthday

c. They like S & M

d. They each were married to the same woman.

10. When Ed "Too Tall" Jones got fed up with his Cowboys salary, he quit the team and took up another sport. What was it?
a. Basketball
b. Hang gliding
c. Boxing
d. Karate
e. Ice dancing

11. How did running back Tony Dorsett celebrate his arrival in Dallas in 1977?
a. He changed the pronunciation of his last name.
b. He signed a big, fat contract.
c. He punched a bartender.
d. He threw a glass at a waitress.
e. All of the above

12. How did the Cowboys react after several former and present players were accused of using drugs?
a. Changed their name to South America's Team.
b. Hired an ex-FBI agent.
c. Showed the team Richard Pryor movies.
d. Got a new team physician.

13. Who was the only NFL player ever to make Roger Staubach cuss during a game?
a. Mel Tom
b. Clint Longley
c. Diron Talbert
d. Conrad Dobler
e. Don Meredith

★ GREAT PLAYS, MEMORABLE MOMENTS ★

A rare find: Tony Dorsett caught holding a football ▲

Real cowboys are great horsemen, right? Right. In 1979, Tony Dorsett was at a bar-be-cue on a ranch in Mount Vernon (hometown of Dandy Don Meredith). Cowboy Tony had his horse fall out from under him, pinning Dorsett to the ground.

"I was just trying to prove to everyone that there are horses in Pennsylvania, too," said Dorsett. "Coal mines isn't all we've got back there."

Witnesses to this great show of horsemanship were struck by the irony: at last something had fumbled Dorsett.

14. What did the Cowboys do with their first draft choice ever?
   a. Drafted Bob Lilly
   b. Traded it to Washington
   c. Drafted Eddie LeBaron
   d. Drafted Don Meredith

15. In 1980, an overzealous Cowboys fan had an unfortunate accident at Texas Stadium while cheering for his team. What happened?
   a. The snowman's costume he was wearing caught fire.
   b. He dressed up as a Cowboys Cheerleader and was propositioned twice.
   c. He tackled Fran Tarkenton in the huddle.
   d. He made a pass at Randy White's wife.

16. Which college has produced the most Dallas Cowboys?
   a. Sam Houston Institute of Technology.
   b. SMU
   c. Texas
   d. Tennessee

17. What was defensive lineman Don Smerek's main injury in 1981?
   a. Slipped disc
   b. Torn cartilage in his knee
   c. Gunshot wound to the abdomen
   d. Herpes

18. How did Tony Dorsett injure himself before the 1979 season?
   a. He was in a car accident.
   b. Hit his head on the bottom of a swimming pool.
   c. Dropped a mirror that a fan gave him and broke his big toe.
   d. Pulled out his wisdom tooth with a pair of pliers.

19. Who was the first Cowboy ever to play in the Pro Bowl?
   a. Eddie LeBaron
   b. Crazy Ray
   c. Bob Lilly
   d. Jim Doran

Like most Cowboys, Crazy Ray can't stand a little kidding.▼

20. Which team holds the record for scoring the most points against the Cowboys in a single game—54?
a. Minnesota Vikings
b. Green Bay Packers
c. TCU Horned Frogs
d. Chippewa Cardinals
e. Hurst Red Raiders

21. In 1980, the Cowboys gained notoriety after their highlight film was entitled "America's Team." What was the name, equally sickening, of the 1981 highlight film?
a. *Next Year's Champions*
b. *Star Spangled Cowboys*
c. *The Big Choke*
d. *God Is a Cowboy*
e. *Hail to the Chief*

22. How many Super Bowls have the Cowboys lost?
a. Three
b. Two
c. None
d. All of them

23. How many NFL title and NFC championship games have they blown?
a. Ten
b. Four
c. Seven
d. Six too few

24. Did Tom Landry have any hair in college? If so, where?

a. No, he had no hair.
b. Yes, but we can't tell you where it was.
c. Yes, on his head.
d. Yes, on his upper lip.

25. Who is the only wife Tom Landry has ever had and how did they meet?
a. Betty—in the hospital.
b. Alicia—on a blind date.
c. Rosita—in Juarez.
d. Gina—in war-torn Italy.

26. Name the college where Tom Landry played football.
a. Slippery Rock
b. Texas A&M
c. Rice
d. University of Texas at Austin

27. What was the name of the first professional team Landry played for?
a. New York Giants
b. New York Yankees
c. New York Titans
d. Dallas Texans

28. Why was former Cowboy quarterback Clint Longley known as "The Mad Bomber?"
a. For slugging Roger Staubach.
b. Because he was in the anti-war movement.
c. For his long touchdown passes.
d. Because he drank too much tequila.
e. Because of the way he hunted rattlesnakes.

29. What is Pete Gent's nickname for Tom Landry?
   a. Smiley
   b. The Old Bomber Pilot
   c. Mr. Warmth
   d. Baldy
   e. Yakamoto Tom

30. Name the football book that the Dallas Cowboys hate the most.
   a. *The Semi-Official Dallas Cowboys Haters' Handbook*
   b. *The Vince Lombardi Story*
   c. *Semi-Tough*
   d. *North Dallas Forty*

31. Name the X-rated movie that the Dallas Cowboys tried to ban.
   a. *Deep Throat*
   b. *Debbie Does Dallas*
   c. *Super Bowl XIII*
   d. *Gay Cowboys*
   e. *Buckaroos in Shoulder Pads*

32. Who scored the first NFL touchdown for a Dallas team?
   a. Frank Clarke
   b. Eddie LeBaron
   c. Buddy Young
   d. Lamar Hunt

33. Which three NFL teams did Clint Murchison try to buy before he got the Dallas franchise (or, put another way, what teams had the good sense not to sell out to him)?
   a. Chicago Cardinals
   b. Canton Bulldogs
   c. Washington Redskins
   d. Kansas City Chiefs
   e. San Francisco 49ers

34. What did Murchison originally want to meet his new NFL expansion team?
   a. Dallas Cowboys
   b. Dallas Buckaroos
   c. Dallas Pistols
   d. Dallas Rangers
   e. Dallas Republicans

35. What former Dallas quarterback once worked in a Nevada law firm with the father of a recent Cowboy quarterback?
   a. Jerry Rhome
   b. Sonny Gibbs
   c. Glenn Carano
   d. Eddie LeBaron

36. Name the Dallas Cowboy who was released by the team shortly after he took Tom Landry Jr. on a snipe hunt during training camp?
   a. Jerry Mallard
   b. Bob Gross
   c. Tom Franckhauser
   d. Billy Clyde Puckett

With the Cowboys' kind of blocking, Jeff and Hazel's little boy had to learn to breathe through his mouth. (AP/Wide World Photos) ▲

37. Who was the first home-grown Dallas Cowboy?
a. Willie Townes
b. J. R. Ewing
c. Guy Reese
d. Texie Waterman

38. How many times was Don Meredith's nose broken in his career?
a. One
b. Seven
c. Fourteen
d. Never

39. How many games did Meredith win in Texas Stadium?
a. Fifteen
b. Six
c. Twenty
d. None

40. Name the American League baseball coach who was once drafted by the Cowboys.
a. Yogi Berra
b. Marv Rettenmund
c. Cal Ripken Sr.
d. Gene Michael

41. Name the former NBA star drafted by the Cowboys in 1966.
a. Willis Reed
b. Lou Hudson
c. Henry Bibby
d. Wilt Chamberlain

Trivia Answers

1. (d) The former New York Yankees franchise moved to Dallas as the Texans. They lost to the Giants, 24–6.

2. (c) 1952.

3. (c) The Cowboys went 0–11–1 in 1960 before winning their first game in 1961.

4. (c) Although Dallas signed Meredith to a personal services contract, the club didn't have any draft choices. So Halas, who was on the NFL expansion committee and lobbied to get a franchise in Dallas, picked Meredith and traded him to the Cowboys.

5. (a) Honest, they once had a drive-in theater.

6. (d) The limos were crowding ordinary fans out of their parking spaces.

7. (a) D. L. Faulkner and his 24-year-old son, Danny, bought the box on the 35-yard line from Dallas County Judge Garry Weber in January 1983. The boxes cost $50,000 when Texas Stadium opened in 1971.

8. (b) Brandt used to hustle baby photos in Milwaukee, Wisconsin hospitals.

9. (d) In this case, Brandt's ex-wife married Murchison.

10. (c) Jones had a 6–0 record against assorted stiffs before he hung up his gloves and returned to football.

11. (e) He was DORsett at the University of Pittsburgh, signed a reported million-dollar contract with the Cowboys and then got in a fight with a Dallas bartender who accused him of not paying for his drinks. The bartender said DorSETT slugged him in the eye, and the waitress said he threw a whisky glass at her.

12. (b) Larry Wansley, known as "Mandrake" because of his disguises, signed as the Cowboys "director of counseling services."

13. (c) We don't know what Roger said to Diron. We can't print what Diron said to Roger.

14. (b) The choice was traded along with a sixth-round pick to the Redskins for quarterback Eddie LeBaron. The Cowboys used their second first-round draft choice in 1961 to take Lilly.

15. (a) Daniel Yoder did his imitation of cherries jubilee during the 1979 playoff game against the Minnesota Vikings after he brushed against a flaming can of Sterno carried by a hot chocolate vendor. He suffered second-degree burns and was taken to the hospital in fair condition.

16. (b and d) Each school has produced 10 Cowboys.

17. (c) Smerek, a reserve, was already injured when he got into a fight in the parking lot of a Dallas nightclub and was shot by an assailant.

18. (c) A fan in Canton, Ohio, gave Dorsett a mirror featuring his likeness. When the nimble running back tried to put it in the overhead baggage compartment on the team bus, he dropped it on his toe. He didn't report the injury until nine days later.

19. (d) Doran, a wide receiver, played only one more

Clint Longley, "The Mad Bomber," lived up to his name on and off the field. ▲

year with the Cowboys after his 1960 Pro Bowl appearance.

20. (a) The slaughter took place in 1970.

21. (b) More flag waving from the Cowboys and NFL Films.

22. (a) To Baltimore in 1970; to Pittsburgh in 1975 and 1978.

23. (c) Only the New York Giants, who have been in the league a lot longer than Dallas, have lost more (11).

24. (c) But not much.

25. (b) Alicia—on a blind date.

26. (d) University of Texas at Austin.

27. (b) The Yankees were in the old All-America Football Conference. He later played for the Giants.

28. (c) He won the nickname after a Thanksgiving Day come-from-behind victory over the Redskins.

29. (b) Landry flew B-17 bombers in World War II. For our side.

30. (d) By Peter Gent. Tex Schramm called it "a total lie."

31. (b) The Cowboys made it hard for Debbie to do Dallas by filing several lawsuits against local theater owners.

32. (c) Young caught a touchdown pass from George Taliaferro on Sept. 28, 1952 for the Dallas Texans.

33. (a, c, e) Murchison even tried to buy the Redskins twice.

34. (d) The team was briefly named the Rangers, but it was changed to Cowboys. Years later, Murchison thought about changing the name of the team again, but fans voted against it.

35. (d) After he retired, LeBaron worked with Glenn Carano's father in a Reno law firm.

36. (b) Landry was not amused.

37. (c) Reese, a defensive lineman for the Cowboys in 1962, played high school football in Dallas and went to SMU. Don Meredith went to SMU, too. But he grew up in Mount Vernon, Texas.

38. (c) And you thought he was just naturally handsome.

39. (d) Meredith retired two years before Texas Stadium opened.

40. (b) Rettenmund, who coached for the Texas Rangers, was drafted by Dallas in the 19th-round in 1965 as a halfback from Ball State.

41. (b) Hudson, a basketball All-America at Minnesota, was the Cowboys' 20th-round draft choice in 1966. He starred with the Atlanta Hawks of the NBA.

Scoring

0–5 correct
—you must be Tom Landry's brother-in-law;

6–15 correct
—you win a tryout with the Redskins;

16–25 correct
—an NFL stadium is named after you;

25+ correct
—you're a genius and should be NFL Commissioner.

THE RING OF DISHONOR

Dallas immortalizes its favorite Cowboys by placing their names in the "Ring of Honor" around Irving's Texas Stadium. Here are a few names you'll never see circling the dome with the hole in the roof.

Lance Rentzel, wide receiver: His infamous down-and-out pattern in front of a little girl earned him a quick trade to Los Angeles. But Lance did learn something in Dallas: how to sell California computers to Republicans.

John Niland, guard: John pulled one time too many. He had a "religious experience" one night in Dallas and began running through the streets speaking in tongues. Several of Dallas' finest were called to the scene before Niland was subdued.

Thomas "Hollywood" Henderson, linebacker: His December 1981 interview in "Playboy" stands as a classic for Cowboys Haters. Henderson was the mouth that roared (See "They Said It") and consistently ended up in Tom Landry's doghouse. The gold star on Henderson's front tooth didn't endear him to Mr. Landry, either.

Nor did his uncanny ability to get up for a game without any words of wisdom from Tom.

Duane Thomas, running back: When Duane was good, he was great. But when he was bad, he was *bad*. Teammates nicknamed Duane "The Sphinx" because he refused to talk. But when "The Sphinx" opened his mouth, out came wisdom, not riddles. He once called Landry, "A plastic man . . . actually, no man at all." That's no way to treat the head coach, Duane. When asked if playing in the Super Bowl was the ultimate experience, he replied, "If it's the ultimate game, why are they playing it again next year?" Thomas thought so much of his Super Bowl ring that he hocked it.

Bob Hayes, wide receiver: Bullet Bob could leave cornerbacks far behind, but he couldn't outrun the law. He was sentenced to five years for possession of cocaine and served nine months before Texas Governor Bill Clements paroled him. The early release prompted Dallas sportswriter Blackie Sherrod to note, "Bob Hayes has proven he's still the world's fastest human by doing a five-year prison sentence in nine months."

Lance Rentzel: Some of his patterns weren't in the playbook. ▲

Bob Hayes—still the world's fastest, with an eye for trouble ▲

Our MPC—Most Prominent Cowboys-Hater

He came out of Michigan State in 1964, a free-spirited free agent who proved to be anything but free.

This basketball player refused the $1,000 signing bonus and told Gil Brandt he wanted a higher salary if he made the team. He made it, and the Cowboys have been paying ever since.

Meet Pete Gent, our MPC—the Most Prominent Cowboys-hater in the world today.

He spent five seasons with the Dallas Corporates and combined recollection with imagination in writing the best-selling *North Dallas Forty*, and, most recently, *The Franchise*. Both were fiction of course, and both dealt with the business side of professional football. The dehumanizing side. The side fans seldom see.

In doing so, Gent hit a few nerves.

Tex Schramm said *North Dallas Forty* was "a total lie. . . . offensive and malicious." He said Gent had "a sick approach to life."

With Schramm voicing such sentiment, you'd think the Cowboys would have purged Pete Gent from any official document.

But the 1983 Cowboys media guide has two references to the man the Cowboys organization loves to hate.

Turn your '83 hymnal to page 82 and you'll find "Gent, Pete" sandwiched between a real cowboy, "Garrison, Walt" and a real disappointment, "Gibbs, Sonny." Fifty-four pages later, under the heading for the Cowboys Longest Plays, an 84-yarder involving Gent and Don Meredith against Pittsburgh on October 30, 1966, still ranks as the eighth-longest pass play in Cowboys history.

A fact that must burn the Cowboys' brass is that Gent joined the Cowboys when they were losers (5–8–1) and left them after the 1968 season, then the team's most

Pete Gent, before and after: Who says football doesn't build character? ▼

successful year (12–2) to date. Much to the chagrin of Schramm and Company, Gent was one of the players that helped turn Dallas from a perennial patsy into a semi-decent football team.

Gent's sin was that he didn't mind talking, or writing, about the not-so-good old days.

So we asked Gent to recall some of the plays and some of the personalities from "the good old days."

Coach Tom Landry and The System

Tom made a lot of mistakes and, remember, in 1964 he wasn't a legend. He was just another coach with a theory and Tom has a pretty good system, but he's not that bright.

When I was playing for them, I said what Landry wanted was eleven strangers on the field and that's what he ultimately got. Eleven strangers. All great athletes. All know The System.

Tom would tell us that you don't have to care about the guy next to you and in his system you really don't. But the problem is, you do have to care about the guy next to you. You have to know who he is and you have to care. Because if you don't it's not sport. What Landry has now are good athletes who think logically like Tom. But you've got to be willing to die for the guys on your side and that's not logical. That's football.

At the end of a game when you're physically getting the s--- beat out of you and you're bleeding and you don't like the coach, logical thinking tells you to just go home and pick up your check because it's going to be the same anyway. Landry has a bunch of guys who look at the point of diminishing returns and realize they shouldn't play any harder. He's finally achieved what he always wanted: eleven strangers.

On Don Meredith

Don has always been underrated. From 1965 to '66, he refused to let Landry call plays and it was a real fight for control of the team. I think more than any one single thing, that made us jump from a 7–7 team in '65 to a 10–3–1 team in '66. We knew we had a leader on the field who had proved himself not only by taking a beating behind a miserable offensive line for years before '66, but when he got control, he wouldn't give it up to anybody. And he didn't give up on any of us on the field. We know when we stepped on the field, we were in it together.

Landry was constantly attacking Meredith because Don faced up to him. Don finally backed off in '67 and it was really the beginning of the end for Don.

On Landry's play calling

I've run in enough plays for Landry to know that he doesn't know what he's calling. It's like the game where you sit in a circle and whisper something off to the right and by the time it comes back to your left ear, it has nothing to do with what you said to the guy on your right.

They call down from the press box and somebody tells Landry and he tells the player and the plays sound similar and then he changes his mind and yells to the player as he's going out onto the field and the guy doesn't hear because everybody is yelling. It's a real mess.

In the 1966 championship game against Green Bay, we lost the game because Landry sent in Bob Hayes on the last play of the game. Hayes had never been in on the goal line [offense] before because we played the split end down tight and used Frank Clarke because he could block. We didn't have any time outs left and in comes Hayes. We try to explain to him what he's supposed to do as we're walking to the line. Hayes was supposed to block [Green Bay's Dave] Robinson for two counts to allow Meredith to roll out. [Hayes didn't block Robinson, who forced Meredith to throw a hurried pass that was intercepted by the Packers in the end zone. Dallas lost, 34–27.]

On Roger Staubach

I always had a lot of respect for Staubach because he could stand in the middle of the field and wait for Landry to send a play in. He had to wonder, 'What in God's name is that idiot gonna send out this time?' I have respect for a guy who can do that. God knows what part of your brain you have to shut off to be able to do that.

On the Cowboys assistant coaches

Remember, it isn't a business overflowing with genius. A guy gets fired in one place and goes to another team as an assistant. And Landry wouldn't want a winning coach, a strong coach as an assistant. When I was with the team, Landry was the receivers coach. He didn't know a thing about teaching us how to run routes. And when we got [former Baltimore star and Hall-of-Famer] Raymond Berry as a receivers coach, he stayed around one year. Landry would never listen to anything he said.

On the Cowboys' policy on political expression

You can't let 'em push you around in your private life. If [Butch] Johnson felt strongly about doing a commercial for Jesse Jackson, he should have done it. Landry did commercials for Reagan. He did commercials for God. Jesus Christ! Landry's going to be selling God, used cars and Jesse Helms.

They Said It

"If they're America's Team, what does that make the rest of us? Guatemalans?"
— *Oakland L.A. Raider safety Mike Davis*

"I think that title gave us a lot more trouble than it was worth."
— *Tom Landry on "America's Team"*

"If Tom Landry and Bud Grant had a personality contest, nobody would win."
— *Don Meredith*

"I don't know. I only played there nine years."
— *Cowboy fullback Walt Garrison, when asked if Tom Landry ever smiles*

"You're one of the two most efficient organizations in the 20th century," television analyst Beano Cook told Cowboys President Tex Schramm.
    "What's the other?" asked Schramm.
    "The Third Reich."

"God, I hate those colors. Pittsburgh's colors look like a steel mill. Dallas's colors remind you of a jewelry store."
— *Anonymous Sportswriter*

"Don't bother reading it, kid. Everybody gets killed in the end."
— *Pete Gent telling a rookie about Tom Landry's playbook*

"If the World Football League succeeds, I'm not going after the players. I want to sign their accountants."
— *Clint Murchison*

"The Cowboys won the Super Bowl last season and I don't see them graduating any seniors."
—*Philadelphia Eagles coach Dick Vermeil on why Dallas was the team to beat in 1977–78. The Cowboys lost the Super Bowl to Pittsburgh.*

"Tex Schramm is a liar, thief and a crook."
—*Cowboy running back Duane Thomas*

"Two out of three isn't bad."
—*Schramm responding to Thomas*

"I don't know what to say. I'm waiting for Coach Landry to send someone in with a statement."
—*Roger Staubach, accepting a Touchdown Club award*

"The higher you climb the flagpole the more people see your rear end."
—*Don Meredith*

"I wouldn't want to be in his position. He doesn't call the plays. He has the responsibility, but not the authority to carry it out."
—*Don Meredith on Danny White*

"If it wasn't for a name like Jethro Pugh, I might be anonymous."
—*Cowboy defensive tackle Jethro Pugh*

"Pittsburgh might have a little better team, but we've got two weeks to get ready. Give Landry two weeks and he'd have beaten Nazi Germany."
—*Cowboy publicist Doug Todd before Super Bowl XIII. Dallas lost, 35–31.*

The Sphinx and the Plastic Man rarely saw eye to eye. ▲

"Bob Hayes has 9.1 speed and 12-flat hands."
—*Otto Graham*

"Landry's system of football is directed in the hope of finally ending up with eleven strangers making up the team, each person knowing the job and the system completely and interacting with his teammates only as specified in the playbook."
—*Pete Gent*

"Would I enjoy going out to dinner with him [Tom Landry]? Sure, why not? As long as Tom chewed his food and wasn't loud and obnoxious to the waiter and behaved himself in a gentlemanly manner, I wouldn't mind at all."
—*Don Meredith*

"I don't know if the Cowboys were the first team to use a computer, but they definitely were the first to brag about it."
—*Former Chicago Bear General Manager Jim Finks*

A good pair beats a full house any day. ◀

"We're good all-American moral Christian women. The organization, I think, epitomizes what life is all about."
—*Dallas Cowboys Cheerleader Melinda May*

"It's not whether you win or lose, but who gets the blame."
—*Cowboy offensive lineman Blaine Nye*

"You could make more money investing in government bonds, but football is more fun."
—*Clint Murchison*

"Terry Bradshaw couldn't spell 'cat' if you spotted him the c and the a."
—*Former Cowboy Thomas "Hollywood" Henderson*

"The NFL will have to adopt a hands-off policy on the cheerleaders."
—*NFL Commissioner Pete Rozelle*

"I still say it's a funny-looking stadium."
—*Don Meredith on Texas Stadium when he was inducted into the Cowboys' sacred Ring of Honor*

"Rooming with Roger Staubach is like rooming with my father."
—*Cowboy linebacker Bob Breunig*

"Dallas used to be beer and nachos. Now it's wine and cheese. Used to be blue jeans; now it's Guccis and Yves St. Laurents."
—*Cowboy receiver Butch Johnson*

"I looked up and thought I saw a picture of Jesus Christ right above the stadium."
—*Cowboy defensive back Dennis Thurman talking about the Cowboys' good luck in a win over Tampa Bay*

"I got sick of hearing about the Cowboys, Cowboys, Cowboys when I was in college. Nobody thinks they can lose. To beat them here means everything."
—*Former SMU All-American and Ram rookie running back Eric Dickerson after LA upset Dallas 24–17 in the 1983 NFC wildcard game*

★ GREAT PLAYS, MEMORABLE MOMENTS ★

In 1969, punter Ron Widby sliced a punt off the side of his foot. As Cowboys and Cardinals tried to avoid touching the bouncing ball, it took a few hops and landed in Widby's hands, making him perhaps the only punter in NFL history to catch his own kick. It was an eight-yard punt. No return.

"Tendencies, man—that's what Landry is all about. He has the response to any tendency in football. Why, Landry does so much research that he know's what George Allen is thinking at night while Allen is sitting alone in his house."
—*Thomas "Hollywood" Henderson*

Hollywood Henderson—a make-things-happen player with a mouth to match ▶

91

"I understand that where little girls used to dream of being Miss America, now they dream of becoming a cheerleader for the Dallas Cowboys."
— *Suzanne Mitchell, director of the Dallas Cowboys Cheerleaders*

"We're going to have to do something about this guy. He's going to ruin the image of an NFL quarterback if he doesn't start smoking, drinking, cussing or something."
— *Don Meredith on Roger Staubach*

★ GREAT PLAYS, MEMORABLE MOMENTS ★

In 1964, the Cowboys set an NFL record for the most times their quarterback was sacked—68 times in one season. No wonder Dandy Don never played in Texas Stadium. Roger Staubach fared little better. In Super Bowl X, Roger was sacked a Super Bowl record seven times by the Steelers.

"His [Staubach's] idea of breaking training is putting whipped cream on his pie."
— *Dallas sportswriter Bob St. John*

"Gentlemen, nothing funny ever happened on a football field."
— *Tom Landry*

"When I think of Dallas, I think of Listerine."
— *Anonymous CBS-TV employee*

"He [Staubach] can play until he's 40 because he doesn't know what a hangover is."
— *Former Redskin quarterback Sonny Jurgensen*

"It seems like by accident you'd get in one of the three times."
— *Tom Landry, on his team's three consecutive losses in NFC championship games. A win would have put the Cowboys in the Super Bowl.*

"I think Texas Stadium is Dallas' attempt to buy a pound of culture and 12 talents."
— *Don Meredith*

"It boils down to one thing: Hate. Hate for reasons that nobody understands."
— *Political satirist Art Buchwald on the intense Washington-Dallas rivalry*

"We feel our personnel is good enough; we just need to be more of a team. The thing we discovered the past two years is that teams can go to the Super Bowl without great experience, as the 49ers proved, and without exceptional talent, as Washington demonstrated."
— *Tom Landry (The "inexperienced" 49ers—1982— and the "unexceptionally talented" Redskins— 1983—beat the Cowboys in the playoffs and went on to win Super Bowls.)*

"George never used to say 'the Dallas Cowboys.' It was always, 'the goddamned Dallas Cowboys.'"
— *Former Cowboy and Redskin John Wilbur on George Allen*

"He was just mad at me all the time because I said quarterbacks are nothing but pussies, which they are."
— *Redskin defensive tackle Diron Talbert on Roger Staubach*

"He probably thought of me as a prima donna."
— *Roger Staubach on Diron Talbert*

"The two most important people to CBS are J. R. Ewing and Tom Landry."
— *Beano Cook*

"I'm used to seeing him like that."
— *Tom Landry on a glassy-eyed Don Meredith after Dandy was tackled hard by the Redskins*

"Just pretend the Cowboys are Iranians."
— *Redskin Diron Talbert on how to get up for a game against Dallas*

"Talk to anyone around the league and they'll tell you, 'We don't care who wins, as long as it isn't the Cowboys.'"
— *Pittsburgh linebacker Jack Lambert*

"Tom Landry is a perfectionist. If he was married to Racquel Welch, he'd expect her to cook."
— *Don Meredith*

"What do you mean, she can't cook?" ▶

"Turn out the lights, the party's over."
—*Don Meredith*

About the Authors

MARK NELSON was born to hate the Cowboys, having been raised in the shadow of the Green Bay Packers in Chippewa Falls, Wisconsin. The seeds for this book were planted during a stint as a reporter for a Texas paper. For fear of reprisal from Dallas Cowboys fans, we won't mention the town or the newspaper. Nelson now plies his trade in our nation's capital surrounded by decent human beings who share his feelings about "America's Team."

MILLER BONNER is a native Texan who grew up idolizing Raymond Berry, Johnny Unitas and Don Meredith. Bonner loved the struggling, expansion Cowboys, but today he is a reformed Dallas Cowboys fanatic. He saw through the hype and hypocrisy and switched his allegiance to the Raiders. Any Raiders. Bonner now lives a few miles east of the Lone Star State and sometimes writes for a living.